THE PATH OF SPIRITUAL HAPPINESS

I0203351

THE PATH OF SPIRITUAL HAPPINESS

Heather M. Erb

 ENROUTE

En Route Books & Media
5705 Rhodes Avenue, St. Louis, MO 63109
Contact us at contactus@enroutebooksandmedia.com
Find En Route online at www.enroutebooksandmedia.com

© En Route Books & Media, 2016

LCCN: 2016954341

Cover design by:
TJ Burdick

The Socrates image featured within inset text boxes is a digital sketch
detail of Jacques-Louis David's "The Death of Socrates" (1787)

All rights reserved. This book, or parts thereof,
may not be reproduced in any form without permission.

Paperback ISBN: 978-1-950108-42-8
E-book ISBN: 978-1-63337-119-4

Printed in the United States of America

THE PATH OF SPIRITUAL HAPPINESS

Heather M. Erb

 ENROUTE

En Route Books & Media
5705 Rhodes Avenue, St. Louis, MO 63109
Contact us at contactus@enroutebooksandmedia.com
Find En Route online at www.enroutebooksandmedia.com

© En Route Books & Media, 2016

LCCN: 2016954341

Cover design by:
TJ Burdick

The Socrates image featured within inset text boxes is a digital sketch
detail of Jacques-Louis David's "The Death of Socrates" (1787)

All rights reserved. This book, or parts thereof,
may not be reproduced in any form without permission.

Paperback ISBN: 978-1-950108-42-8
E-book ISBN: 978-1-63337-119-4

Printed in the United States of America

CONTENTS

To my family—a little school of virtue

I hope that this book adds a stone to the apologetic tower of truth, and helps all who read it rejoice in St. Thomas's saying, that it is impossible that God, as the essence of beauty & goodness, be seen without love.

FOREWORD

Recent times have witnessed a resurgence of interest in the importance of a distinctively Catholic education. This resurgence of interest is due in no small measure to a realization that contemporary education has lost its way, having become beholden to economic and political interests. Naturally, when economic and political interests loom large on the educational scene, the human person in all his/her dignity is displaced. Unfortunately, even traditionally Catholic educational institutions have not been immune from these corrosive developments.

This state of affairs has spawned a serious reflection on the nature and role of education. Among those who have written on the subject of education in the last number of years are intellectual luminaries such as Alasdair MacIntyre, Reinhard Hütter, and Benedict M. Ashley, OP—not to mention Popes John Paul II and Benedict XVI. The renewed interest has not been limited to the domain of speculative philosophy and theology. It has also expressed itself practically in the foundation of a host of new Catholic educational institutions in the USA.

The role of philosophy and theology in genuine Catholic education, however, is and will always remain indispensable. It would, however, be a mistake to think that the particular content and structure of the philosophical curriculum is of no real consequence, just as it would be a grave error to think that it is as educationally valuable to teach heterodox theology to young students as it is to ground them in the demands of Catholic orthodoxy. Indeed, the implications of philosophy for the life of faith and theology are momentous: one's philosophical perspective will largely dictate where one goes theologically. Much if not all dissent from the magisterium of the Catholic Church is not due to any malice whatsoever. It is due simply to a seriously defective philosophical formation.

Let me be clear. I do not for one moment advocate a refusal to engage with different philosophical and theological opinions. Such engagement is crucial and can often be illuminating. Sound pedagogy, however, dictates that educators do not adopt this kind of engagement as their starting-point. Firm intellectual foundations have to be laid before meaningful engagement with other philosophical and theological traditions and opinions is possible. Otherwise one will inevitably sow yet more seeds of the kind of widespread confusion we witness in today's world. Insofar as Catholic education is concerned, this confusion is due in no small part to the departure in all too many institutes of higher learning from the Aristotelian-Thomistic philosophical synthesis. With regard to the theme of this present book this realist philosophy teaches us a simple yet crucial lesson: if the human quest for happiness is to be realized in any way at all in this life then it must respect the structure of reality in general and of human nature in particular.

And yet reason on its own is not enough. Faith is also required. As John Paul II writes in *Fides et Ratio*, "with the light of reason human beings can know which path to take, but they can follow that path to its end, quickly and unhindered, only if with a rightly tuned spirit they search for it within the horizon of faith" (*FR* 16). He concludes that "reason and faith cannot be separated without diminishing the capacity of men and women to know themselves, the world and God in an appropriate way" (ibid.). If I may express the point more provocatively: the highest level of intelligence insofar as the pursuit of true happiness is concerned, is reserved for those who are enlightened by the light of the one, true, holy, and apostolic faith. Such faith and such intelligence are necessarily ecclesial in character and consequently presuppose fidelity to the Church's Magisterium.

This synthesis of faith and reason and fidelity to the Church's magisterium is a hallmark of this present volume which deals with the most fundamental of human desires, namely the desire for happiness. It presents the reader with a highly lucid treatment of an array of issues relevant to a correct understanding of its true nature by engaging with the thought of Aristotle and St. Thomas Aquinas as well as with that of Josef Pieper, one of the most celebrated interpreters of St. Thomas. Indeed, each of the three parts offers a supremely fine introduction to the reflections on happiness of each of these thinkers. Judicious references to *Fides et Ratio* and *Veritatis Splendor*, two of John Paul II's most important encyclicals on the relationship between faith and reason and on moral philosophy and theology respectively, afford the reader a clear sense of how faith and reason both cohere with each other and illuminate the path to genuine happiness in this life and to its fulfilment in final beatitude in the next life.

Heather Erb has done all who are interested in the furtherance of Catholic education—both within official institutions and beyond—a great favour in penning the following pages. The great Dominican moral theologian, Servais Pinckaers, highlighted the fact that happiness is at the core of the authentic Christian moral tradition right from the very beginning. In an age in which we are assailed on all sides by anti-contemplative relativistic and atheistic philosophies, she has provided a highly accessible resource for professors and their students. This resource illuminates the essential components of the quest for happiness in terms of the intellectual framework that has to date proved itself more suitable than any other—namely realist philosophy illumined by the light of the Catholic faith. The insights and guidance afforded by any other approach, if they not be in fact harmful, cannot match the power of this venerable synthesis.

I am honoured to have been asked to contribute the foreword to this book. My own desire is that it become a standard text in Catholic educational circles and, indeed, beyond! In my estimation this short treatise on happiness, largely philosophical but one which "responds to the challenge of theology's demands and evolves in harmony with faith" (*FR* 103) is a shining example of philosophy in the service of the new evangelization. What better way to prepare the soil of contemporary culture for the reception of the Gospel of Joy than to outline the nature of true happiness!

Kevin E. O'Reilly, OP
Angelicum University
Rome

PREFACE

Inspired by St. Augustine and the Scriptures, St. Thomas Aquinas says in his *Compendium of Theology* (II.9) that we pine for the joy that crowns human beatitude. In this joy we also find the beauty of peace which is a wealthy rest or abundance of all goods, to be found only by seeing the Truth.

In thinking through the issues in this book, I became convinced that our search for true happiness finds its home in Christian philosophy. Plato and Aristotle's thought, I discovered, provided the soil from which the seeds of an authentic Christian wisdom sprouted, with Aristotle's strong light of realism lending a rich atmosphere of warmth and clarity. This preparation enabled supremely gifted thinkers like St. Thomas and his follower, Catholic philosopher Josef Pieper, to harvest reason's fruits for grace and glory.

Our perfect and ultimate happiness will have no fellowship with the darkness of corruptible things, for by grace, we are being led into the changeless abundance of all goods in the enjoyment of God. St. Thomas's uplifting paean to the Cause of our beatitude is truly a chant of thanksgiving for the Good in all our goods Who draws us through knowledge and love into complete serenity, security, and the peace that endures forever.

St. Thomas thus develops his philosophy as an explorer seeking eternity, with a holy ardor whose light shines through Athens, but whose source is in Jerusalem. As the British poet laureate Robert Bridges once exclaimed, "every gentle heart that burns with true desire, is lit from eyes that mirror part of that celestial fire."

An unmistakable Thomist genius infuses the thought of Pope John Paul II, who, as both a theologian and a philosopher, scrutinizes our modern (and postmodern) predicament as a context for exploring the proper roles of reason and faith, freedom and the natural and divine laws. With prophetic accuracy, he warns us of the disastrous effects of the gulf between Christian wisdom and failed modern philosophies in his encyclicals *Fides et Ratio* and *Veritatis Splendor*.

The idea for the content and style of this book stems from an immensely enjoyable interactive online course I taught for Catholic philosophy and theology students. I owe Robert Royal thanks for his insightful comments on an earlier version of this text. Also, I thank my various students through the years for incarnating the great truth that it is philosophy's job not to explain mysteries away eloquently by reference to "reality," but to find and love that Reality on whose presence everything depends, and hold fast to It in our delightful stammering.

INTRODUCTION

St. Thomas Aquinas, fed by the streams of Biblical revelation and the wisdom of Aristotle, left no area of our common human experience outside the radiance of divine love. In this, he is a great friend on our road to happiness. He kept company with Aristotle's searching mind, pondering whether our happiness is a matter of human effort, divine dispensation, or just plain luck. All the while, his heart embraced the wise counsel of faith, which pointed his intellect towards greater frontiers.

As the humble friar toiled, prayed, and occasionally wept along the rugged road of study and virtue, he knew with St. Augustine (and in our time, C. S. Lewis) that the way to beatitude is often blocked not because we desire too much, but rather because we desire far too little. We are too easily pleased with that which ultimately fades or dissolves beside the undiluted eternity we seek!

Shadowy counterfeits such as fleeting pleasure, complex satisfactions sought through artificial techniques, chemical panaceas, entertainment, and even personal achievements, ultimately fail in strength and beauty before the immortality that is our destiny. Often, he who follows his *grande passion* fails, and if he succeeds, he is the sadder for it. Why? Ephemeral, partial goods are simply unable to quench our thirst for infinite love and ultimate truth. As the philosopher-mystic St. John of the Cross wisely noted, "love (viz., the wound of love) is not cured save by things in harmony with love" (*Spiritual Canticle* II.11). The consciousness of our drive for ultimate goodness, truth, and beauty cannot help but be pressing and perplexing, since it surges from the deepest part of ourselves.

Glimpses of the joy that lies beyond this world often hit us by sur-prise—in the dappled sunlight splashing through the forest; in the sound of a screen door and voices on a summer's eve; or in an unexpected chord that makes us shiver with mysterious delight. Yet we must be tuned in to see and to listen, in order to receive those moments of grace, those brushes with spiritual happiness.

Further, we must be tested and formed in the human wisdom that opens into grace, that light which silently guides our footsteps. St. Thom-as and his twentieth century Thomist follower Josef Pieper rejoiced that Providence led the Greek philosophers (and in particular Aristotle, whose thought St. Thomas "baptized") to investigate our human landscape with their irresistible power and precision, even though as pagans, they could not taste the full sweetness of their quarry.

In this book, we first turn to the Greek philosopher Aristotle (Part One) to help us (as every wise man will) make an order in life. The "Phi-losopher," as St. Thomas fondly called him, was, along with Socrates and Plato, one of the early pioneers who cleared a path for man towards happi-ness. Aristotle saw our ultimate horizon as basically natural, or this-world-ly. But since our human natures are made for excellence in thought and action, we are also guided by a divine element in our "forms" or souls, for which we should strain and sacrifice all. The Greek's deep understanding of the human person provided later Christian philosophers with important tools for the high adventure of sanctity, including the nobility of goodness which bases the later religious idea of friendship with God.

Aristotle likens us to archers who must find the target (our goal or "*telos*") before we release the arrow (our chosen actions), and like athletes in the Olympic Games, who win not by sheer beauty or even by power (or by having the newest smart phone!), but by rushing out onto the field of life. We must *participate* in life, forging our well-chosen spiritual happiness through developing the virtues—those habits of mind and heart which help secure the "basic goods" of a flourishing human life.

Human dignity requires that these goods transcend mere bodily survival, even though as animals, we require pleasure to learn and grow. The values of friendship, justice, knowledge, and contemplation of the highest things define his ethics to be less a rule book or moral straightjacket than a spiritual powerhouse that fuels excellence of character and intellect through an alert, persevering and joyful self-mastery.

St. Thomas Aquinas (Part Two) broadened and deepened the philosophy of Aristotle by peacefully insisting, against the cacophony of modern voices, that our desire for happiness signals our identity as creatures made in the image of a generous personal God. This key insight is the pivot on which our beatitude turns, since it extends the gift of happiness from its Greek origins in the few privileged elite who are capable of an array of virtues through broad worldly experience, and gives it to all of us *rustici* (country dwellers) who, like peasants, must beg for our spiritual food as we wander through the lands this side of heaven.

St. Thomas enlists philosophy as the "handmaid" of theology to illumine the landmarks of moral and intellectual virtue, pleasure, friendship, and well-tuned passions, along the path to happiness. God's invitation to communion with Him sweeps us into His design for all creation, beyond the faltering steps and closed systems of the philosophers and the muted material delights of mere worldlings. Our consciousness of this invitation often surprises us in unexpected moments of grace, like a tumbling cascade of water frothing up from unseen depths of rock.

Echoing the Dominican saint's Biblical inspiration and held firm by St. Thomas's anchor St. Augustine, Pope John Paul II emphasizes the role of freedom and the divine law as a context for understanding St. Thomas's hierarchically structured vision of the road to beatitude, from nature to grace, to glory.

In Part Three, we turn to the twentieth century interpreter of St. Thomas, Josef Pieper, to explore the link between happiness, leisure, philosophy and worship. In our time, when the temptation of ersatz happiness in the form of self-anesthetizing techno-hedonism is pervasive, Pieper's thesis that authentic culture is based on the "activity" of true leisure as expressed through the love of wisdom stands as an invitation to the recovery of Western civilization and sanity. It is in transcendent activities such as the splendor of Christian philosophy that culture survives and flourishes. Most importantly, authentic culture is secured and directed by its vital link with divine worship, which affirms creation as "festival" and calls us to respond in gratitude, intelligence, and love.

The dialogue of faith and reason and the high adventure of the moral life are explored in John Paul II's encyclicals *Fides et Ratio* and *Veritatis Splendor*, which provide the context for the interplay between philosophy and our human destiny. Anti-contemplative relativistic and atheistic philosophies pervert the glorious music of reason into a weapon ultimately destructive of human nature itself.

Faith teaches us that we walk beneath God's gaze and expect the fulfillment of a promise. It also guarantees what John Paul II calls the "affective rectitude" needed for reason to excel (*Fides et Ratio* #16-#18). John Paul II, like Josef Pieper, preserves the integrity of human reason, while re-grafting it onto its divine source, in the recognition that the simplest and deepest truth about ourselves, the heart of our life and the basis for all fine action, lies in the relation of God to our soul.

But what does the grandeur of beatitude have to do with life on earth, for the ordinary person? How can it guide us in our interactions with an aggressive, shallow society and its humanist idols of worldly gain and glory? And, shouldn't happiness have its prelude here below, at least for the just ones seeking truth?

Faith calls us to joyfully challenge the world in which we are placed. But meeting a secular, atheistic world involves setting out on an adventure (Tolkien would say, beyond the Shire!) with the help of realist philosophy, a trusty guide which helps us make clear distinctions, recognize the landmarks, and, ultimately, address the ailments of modern culture. If the pattern of Christian philosophy prevailed in our lives, we would never be left without two companions: First, the natural, human virtue growing out of good choices and philosophical wisdom, and second, the shining supernatural virtue breathed forth from grace, propelling and inspiring us towards intimacy with God. In contrast to the atheist critiques so aptly lamented by John Paul II, which claim the illusory quality and irrelevance of faith, the demands of Christian happiness actually insert us in the very heart of the world, infusing it with the fruits of our contemplation.

Even if our complete happiness is deferred to the afterlife in the beatific vision, this does not excuse us from vigorously pursuing the moral life here on earth. After all, our intellects and wills are the formative causes guiding the pursuit of happiness in our personal lives, our families and our society.

This book is intended as a self-guided study or teaching tool to introduce Christian philosophy. I offer it in the spirit of friendship to all searching for their true homeland, and in the hope that the wealth of Christian wisdom might once again become an unrelenting form of life among believers.

Heather M. Erb
Little Lake Joseph, Ontario, Canada
August, 2016

—PART ONE—
Aristotle's Theory of Happiness

Aristotle, detail from *The School of Athens* by Raphael

REFLECTION

"Happiness then is the best, noblest, and most
pleasant thing in the world."

(Aristotle, *Nicomachean Ethics* I.8)

"We must strain every nerve to live in accordance with the best
thing in us; for even if it be small in bulk, much more does it in
power and worth surpass everything."

(Aristotle, *Nicomachean Ethics* X.7)

In contrast to moral relativism, Aristotle's ethics is based on the universal characteristic of human nature, namely, reason. In this section, we discover how Aristotle establishes an objective end of human nature common to all persons. Human happiness, known as flourishing or "eudaimonia," he says, involves an exercise of virtue whose seeds are inscribed in our nature. Happiness consists in various bodily, external, and spiritual goods, and is directed towards the perfection of the contemplative life. In this section, we also discuss the roles of pleasure and friendship in happiness, and ask why the Christian philosopher cannot embrace Aristotle's ethics of human flourishing without reservation.

The *Catechism of the Catholic Church* explains that human dignity is rooted in our status as beings made in the Image of God (Part III, 1700-1706). Our nature, therefore, can only be fulfilled in the way that, by our free choices, we direct ourselves to communion with the Creator, who is both the source of our being and the goal of our life. The principles that guide us in these choices form what is usually called moral theology. The Catholic tradition draws on many sources, but in moral questions, it is particularly rooted in the thought of the ancient Greek philosopher Aristotle (384-322 B.C.) and the additions, adaptations, and explanations of Aristotle brilliantly carried out by St. Thomas Aquinas (1225-1274 A.D.). The more than 1,500 years that separates these two great thinkers, and the way their thought has survived into the twenty-first century, confirms the durability of certain moral notions.

In this section, we will look at a number of common topics in Catholic moral philosophy. These are first, the relation of human desires and inclinations to our ultimate happiness; second, the metaphysics of moral choice as rooted in rationality and freedom; and third, virtue as a "habit" directed towards the fulfillment of human nature.

These and many other characteristically Catholic notions find their origin in Aristotle. As a first approach to our subject, we will identify this background to Aquinas's theory of happiness. Then, we will explore how Christianity provides a somewhat different perspective on those ideas and adds to them. As you will see, Aristotle arrived at a profound natural understanding of the human person; Catholic thought completes that understanding by showing how beatitude is our ultimate destiny and the difference this makes even to living good lives in this world.

CHAPTER ONE
Aristotle and Philosophy

To begin our topic of Aristotle's theory of happiness, we must know how Aristotle's thought stands in relation to his chief influence, Plato (428-348 B.C.), and in relation to the Christian moral theology that followed. Aristotle is the Greek philosopher famous for dividing knowledge into its basic categories of science, logic, philosophy and literature. Much that Aristotle wrote has been lost, but what survives are edited technical works thought to be lecture notes of Aristotle and his students from his school, the Lyceum. The contribution of Aristotle to philosophy can be viewed from two perspectives. First, we can approach his thought in relation to that of his master Plato. Second, we can study it as a preparation for the medieval debates on the nature of the soul, beatitude and ethics, and the relationship between faith and reason in the thirteenth century, as taken up by St. Thomas Aquinas. In the course of this chapter, we shall touch upon both aspects, thus illumining the contributions of ancient and medieval philosophy to Catholic moral theology as found in the *Catechism*.

Taking the first perspective, it is well known that Plato continued the tradition set by his teacher Socrates (470-399 B.C.) of challenging commonly held (but poorly developed) ideas concerning the nature of the soul, human community and reality itself. For both men, to be a philosopher or "lover of wisdom" (*philo-sophos*) meant a readiness to detach oneself from the popular mind and to rethink the foundations of our knowledge and actions. Inhabiting a world not unlike our own in its emphasis on appearances and the pursuit of pleasure, Plato followed his master by challenging the great theatre of sophistry that is the world. He did this by overturning the "common sense" materialist view of reality, exchanging the full-fledged reality of the physical world for an invisible unchanging world of "Forms" or "Ideas" on which physical things are modeled or patterned, and in whose pure reality things are said to imitate and share. These "Forms" were later adapted by St. Augustine (354-430 A.D.) into the archetypes in God's mind by which things are created, the "divine Ideas." In accord with his view on the Forms, Plato considered the soul to be immaterial and immortal, and held up a purely abstract notion of goodness ("the Good") to govern his ethics. The practice of philosophy was likened to the "swan song," a poignant meditation whereby the soul is gradually drawn away from the material world and summoned to its home in eternity after its separation from the body.

> Plato's dialogue, the *Phaedo*, depicts the trial of his master Socrates, sometimes called the "first Christian," although he was a holy pagan living before Christ. Unlike the later arid, technical discussions of philosophers, Socrates linked the love of wisdom ("philosophy") with a life well-lived, which is illustrated in his own "swan song" in which Socrates guides us through the last and most joyful day of his earthly life.
>
>
>
> "When these birds feel that the time has come for them to die, they sing more loudly and sweetly than they have sung in all their lives before, for joy that they are going away into the presence of the god whose servants they are."
>
> (*Phaedo* 84E)

Because philosophy focuses on eternal realities, it is a "rehearsal for death," or the beginning of the separation of our souls from our bodies, and a celebration of our return to our eternal home. Plato gave Catholic philosophy the concept of the immaterial and immortal soul, the notion of philosophy as a search for truth, goodness and beauty, and the outlines of a notion of a transcendent God who is the source of all being. Aristotle's contributions lay more in the direction of the foundations of the moral life, the metaphysics of the human person (philosophical anthropology) and the nature of human knowledge.

An avid student of the physical world around him, Aristotle respected the reality of each material living thing, taking the job of philosophy to be the pursuit of truth through the classification of the sciences. Unlike Plato, he viewed the soul as closely bound to the body in its activities of knowing and loving, and not immortal. We define things, Aristotle says, by means of their actions, not by means of some abstract unseen "Idea" they represent. For example, a man is a "rational animal," since he uses his mind and also uses his five senses. So also in ethics, morality is something concrete, not abstract. What matters is *acting* in a good way, not just *knowing* what is good. Socrates said that one would *do* the right thing if one only *knew* what it was, but Aristotle understood weakness of will, and in this sense was more useful to later Christians in developing their theories of morality. His thought reached Christian theologians of the thirteenth century in a roundabout way through the Arab world, where his scientific works had been studied. It was through St. Thomas Aquinas that Christianity would adopt many of Aristotle's ideas, including insights about the union of the soul and the body (*hylemorphism*), about the structure of reality in terms of material and immaterial components, and about the virtues, the value of friendship and contemplation. Perhaps surprisingly, it was Aristotle's philosophy that provided pieces of the Christian theology of grace, as found in theories of the sacraments, the virtues, charity, the Church and the limits of human reason.

Discussion Questions:

1. What were the contributions of the Greek philosophers to Christian philosophy, especially ethics?

2. Why is theorizing only one step in the achievement of happiness, for Aristotle?

Readings:

In addition to Pope John Paul II's encyclicals (*Fides et Ratio; Veritatis Splendor*), there are readings to accompany the chapters (Note: *NE* I.1-2 = Aristotle's *Nicomachean Ethics*, Book 1, chapters 1-2).

*   Plato: *Phaedo;* Aristotle: *Meta.* II.1; *NE* VI.2

CHAPTER TWO
Thinking, Doing and Making:
The World of *Ends* and *Means*

We use our minds in many ways in the course of a day, even if we are not reflecting on the fact. We think about everything from possibilities of action and about theories put forward in books we read, to what to make for dinner. We can think about our headache, about how to do the "just" thing today, or about the effortless scales of a Mozart sonata. On the other hand, we can think about the *purpose* of pain, about "justice" as a general *idea* and about the *nature* of beauty. Aristotle distinguished three basic ways of knowing, which scholars know as our dimensions as "man the knower" (*speculative thinking*) "man the doer" (*practical thinking*) and "man the maker" (*productive thinking*). We think theoretically or *speculatively* in our pursuit of *truth* as "man the knower" (Aristotle's works on *science* and *theoretical philosophy*). We think *practically* as moral and social beings in our pursuit of *happiness* (*the good*) as "man the doer" (his works on *politics* and *ethics*). We think *productively* in our pursuit of *beauty* and *utility* as "man the maker" (Aristotle's works on the *arts*). When we think about our ultimate destiny as humans, what we are thinking about is happiness, according to Aristotle. To obtain our goal of being happy is a *practical good*, because it is something we want to *do and enjoy*, not just know about. It is by studying ethics that we come to know in what our happiness consists, and come to know *how to get there.*

Goals are called **ends**; ways of reaching goals are called **means**. Building a house is a goal, hiring a contractor to build it is a means. Building a house may *also* be a means to a further goal, such as selling it for profit. In practical thinking, Aristotle says, the process of *establishing goals or ends* cannot go on forever. Even if we don't usually think about an "ultimate" goal of life *explicitly*, this goal is still the motivation underlying all that we do. We build a house to turn a profit, to obtain funds to go to the Italian Riviera and relax. In short, we build a house in order to be happy. Happiness, however we conceive of it, is the final goal of living. Without an *ultimate goal/end*, there is nothing to motivate action. It is the purpose of ethics to determine what the real goal of life is, and to provide us with a story of how to get there—a story in which we play the main characters.

Discussion Questions:

1. Why is happiness an end, and not a means to something else?

2. Why does Aristotle think we act towards an "ultimate end"?

Readings:

• *NE* I.1; 8

CHAPTER THREE
Wants, Needs and Virtues

The *end* or *goal* of human life is what fulfills us, makes us happy, and what is *good* for us. This is why the "good" has the character of an end (*telos*). The good is what all things *desire*, and all things aim at some good (*NE* I.1). Even at the lowest level of nature, we see things moving towards the perfection of their natures (trees growing, etc.). We cannot imagine someone *not* desiring what they *think* is *good* in some way. Even the most flagrant sinner desires something he *perceives* as good, in the sense of being pleasing to him. But everyone knows that we should avoid things that are not *actually* good for us. It is only our *complete and true perfection* as *human beings* that should steer us through life and be the object of our desires. From this, we see that there are many senses of the term *good* for Aristotle:

1. *real* versus *apparent* good
2. *external* goods, *bodily* goods, and *spiritual* goods
3. *metaphysical* versus *moral* good

First, something can be *really or truly good* for us (the *basic goods,* which are our human *needs*), or only *apparently good* for us (human *wants*). **Second,** there are goods that we can *possess*, which are *external goods* (such as wealth), goods we can physically *experience*, which are *bodily goods* (such as health), and goods that we can *achieve* (which are *spiritual goods* such as knowledge and moral virtue). *Spiritual goods* are said to *perfect* us in that they actualize our higher capacities—to live in truth and goodness. Just as the body is perfected by exercise, so the soul is perfected when it knows the truth and loves the good. Aristotle calls this perfection an *excellence* or *virtue*—the "intellectual virtues" perfect our mind; the "moral virtues" perfect our will—our appetite for personal wholeness and balance which is sated only by something completely good.

In our search for happiness, we should seek to *want* only what we *need* and not want things inordinately. It is good to want drink, but not necessarily an entire bottle of Grand Marnier. It is good to want to eat, but not necessarily a box of truffles for breakfast. It is good to want to play, but not at the expense of passing an exam. The "basic goods" of human life are a complex unity corresponding to our complex humanity; a balanced unity of lower goods, such as food and sleep, permitting the achievement of higher spiritual goods such as knowledge, virtue and friendship.

Thomas Aquinas was to build on Aristotle's theory and present a system of "natural law" based on the basic inclinations of human nature (*Summa Theologiae* I-II 94.2). For both philosophers, human nature represents less a denial or limitation of human freedom, than a foundation for it. Without human nature, warns Pope John Paul II in *Veritatis Splendor* #46 (1993), "man would be nothing more than his own freedom," which in turn becomes "self-defining and a phenomenon creative of itself and its values." This leads to the lived contradiction of attempting to forge our humanist-style "personal life project" without the foundation of our own humanity!

Mortimer Adler is one writer who explains Aristotle's text by dividing our desires into the things we **need** (*innate* or *natural desires*) and the things we merely **want** (*acquired desires*). Studying ethics leads us to an explicit knowledge of the human *needs* whose fulfillment constitutes our happiness, and helps us avoid misery by learning to "line up" our *wants* with our actual *needs.*

> *NEED* (*innate/natural desire*)
> a) known to us (physical needs: nutrition)
> b) not always known explicitly (spiritual needs: knowledge, community, play, worship, etc.)

Desire: ••

> *WANT* (*acquired, specific desires*)
> a) physical (e.g.caviar, champagne)
> b) spiritual (e.g.joining a certain club)

The ***third*** division within goodness is between *metaphysical* and *moral* goodness. A thing is *metaphysically good* when it has all that it needs to act according to its nature. In this way, a tree is good which has leaves or needles. A car is good whose transmission is working. An *action* is *morally good,* on the other hand, when it helps us attain our final end, our happiness (and conversely, it is *morally bad* when it takes us off that road).

The etymology of the word *virtue* is the Latin *vir,* meaning a *man,* and has its roots in warfare. What the Romans took as strength of character in adversity, the Greeks took as excellence of character, *arête.* Virtue is an excellence or perfection that makes a thing function well. This strange sense of virtue (*arête*) applies to both the *metaphysical* and the *moral* levels of goodness. An excellent knife cuts well; an excellent person reasons and acts well. A person can possess both *intellectual* virtues (perfections of his mind, such as *science*), and *moral* virtues (such as *temperance or moderation; courage; honesty* and so on). The *moral virtues* help us reach excellence or function well as humans, through guiding our *actions* and our *emotions* towards the good. The *moral vices* drag us away from our vocation to nobility, even though they may provide momentary pleasure. The *intellectual virtues* span the entirety of our knowing, from applied and technical knowledge, to the prudence of good action, and carry us towards our destiny, the sublimity of wisdom about God.

Discussion Questions:

1. What are the various meanings of "good" and which one(s) concern happiness? How?

2. Do you think it's important to distinguish "wants" and "needs"? Why?

Readings:

•   *NE* I.2; III.4

CHAPTER FOUR
What *is* "Happiness"?

At this stage we have gotten the hint that happiness has something to do with virtue. Aristotle's term for happiness is *eudaimonia*, which has been translated variously as "happiness," "flourishing" and "success." It might seem illogical and unfair that the nature of the most important goal in life (happiness) needs to be uncovered by study. But unlike the philosophers and pundits of today, Aristotle had great confidence in the power of human reason to unveil the truth about things, and in the openness and availability of truth to our minds. The *realism* that pervades his ethics makes way for the Incarnation that respects both the nobility and earthly quality of fragile human nature. But without a clear sense of divine Providence and immortality, Aristotle saw happiness as achievable only by the privileged few and surpassed by death itself.

Many identify happiness as the life of *pleasure*, the life of *honor* or the life of *wealth,* intuiting that these goods make life better in some way. But happiness must be more inclusive, more durable and less subject to chance and to loss than any of these goods. We are not happy in the same way that animals are contented; we are "masters" of our actions who can control our attitudes when we cannot always control external circumstances (an insight later Stoics were to adopt). The popular views of happiness present too narrow a picture of human fulfillment and ignore the important fact that we can, to an important extent, design a life of virtue amidst the vicissitudes of life. Building a life of virtue is a graceful if precarious art, not the kind of psychological warfare and manipulative tactics envisioned by proponents of "positive thinking," who view happiness as a drug or commodity created by the channeling of "positive energy" towards ourselves.

In fact, Aristotle anticipates the Church's insistence on the indissoluble link between freedom, truth and goodness. In Pope John Paul II's affirmation of Church teaching in *Veritatis Splendor* (#84), we see the Greek's teaching adapted to fit the Christian view that "only the freedom which submits to the Truth leads the human person to his true good. The good of the person is to be in the Truth and to *do* the Truth."

In some ways Aristotle also resembles the philosopher Kant, who spoke of the *human will* as the only truly good thing on earth, a jewel that shines by its own light—a far cry from a life driven by mere physical satisfaction, transitory wealth and power, or the accolades of others. Aristotle saw happiness in the life of moral and intellectual perfection of our soul, which requires interiority or inner order. While the effects of virtue overflow into our family and society, happiness is fundamentally an *immanent or interior activity*—one could say that the "home" of happiness is the soul, not the life of busy-ness and distractions that is the norm today.

Aristotle lists *two criteria* that help us define "happiness"(*NE* I.7). It must be both *final* (not a means to something else, like buying a house) and *self-sufficient* (taken on its own, it makes life worthwhile—no single good, such as wealth or power, could fit this bill; only a good that includes all others—what Aquinas would call the "universal good" [*bonum universale*]). He then defines **happiness** as:

> ... an activity of the soul in conformity with virtue (*arête*), and
> if there are several virtues, then in conformity with the best and
> most complete. (1098a16-18)

Eudaimonia is neither a passive, fleeting *emotional* state ("did that movie make you *happy*?"), nor is it an *innate quality* (like eye color), nor a matter of *luck* ("winning the lottery made me *happy*"). It is not just *having* virtues but *exercising* them. It is an activity of the soul (for bodies may be rested or healthy but not "happy"), and if there is a highest excellence or perfection of our soul, it must involve that. Aristotle does admit that luck is *part* of our happiness, in a preparatory way. We cannot be happy if we are ugly, poor, sick, childless, or barbarian, for instance. Fortunately, Aristotle's Athenian elitism is tempered by a strong emphasis on the ability of humans to *overcome* circumstances, for he speaks of a wise general who uses whatever soldiers and equipment are at his disposal to win the battle. In addition to being *final* and *self-sufficient,* and involving both *reason* and *moral virtue, eudaimonia* is an activity practiced in a *complete life*, for one swallow does not make a spring any more than a short time makes one happy (I.7). Aristotle's "happy life" is like a musical duet animated alternately by acts of *moral* and *intellectual* virtue, sometimes darkened by a minor key and mysteriously hushed at death.

When we turn to the nature of the *intellectual virtues* in Book VI and to the topic of "contemplation" in Book X.7-8, we see Aristotle straining to supply us with a description of the "highest virtue" of wisdom (*sophia)* that is the summit of our life. He notes that our highest achievement as humans is "contemplation" — something performed by our "highest power" exercised on the "highest object." What he is getting at is a decidedly philosophical kind of correlation. Something is perfect insofar as it is not subject to decay and change. The background of this thinking goes as follows: When something changes, it changes for good or worse. If for good, it was not perfect but it needed something *more*. If for worse, it was not perfect since its goodness was subject to loss, being possessed in a transitory way. Take a painting, for example. The artist can add a finishing touch or paint over an error. A thing is imperfect when it can change, or when it can decay. An apple decays when separated from the tree; a human body is subject to disease and decay.

In his book *The Physics*, Aristotle argued that there must be some "first cause" of the universe to provide the impetus for all the motions of physical beings, even of the planets. This first cause (actually, he saw them as several), the Unmoved Mover, is *immutable—not* subject to change or decay and can't be perfected or made more complete by *adding* something or by *taking something away.* It is perfect because it is simple, pure immateriality—for something without material parts cannot be dissolved or destroyed. You can't pull it apart like sections of an orange; you see things reflected in it, like light; perhaps this is why Aristotle refers to the intellect as the most "godlike" or divine element in us (X.7-8; both Plato, Augustine, Aquinas and the medievals used the imagery of "light" to illustrate divinity). So, in this section of the *Ethics* we see the beginnings of St. Thomas Aquinas's concepts of God, immortality and the beatific vision.

Discussion Questions:

1. What is happiness for Aristotle, and how does it differ from some popular ideas of happiness in Aristotle's day, and in today's Western culture?

2. Why is happiness connected to the idea of "the good," and isn't just blind optimism, on the one hand, or a fleeting emotion, on the other?

Readings:

- *NE* I.4-5; 7-8; X.7-8

CHAPTER FIVE
Moral and Intellectual Virtues

When virtue is possessed, it is lodged in the soul like the sap in a tree. When the sap is healthy, the fruit of the moral life is produced; when the sap is running, the sweetness of beatitude can flow forth. The seat of virtue is the soul, which is a complex of vegetable, animal and rational functions (I.13). We have all experienced our reason and free will governing the emotions and instincts, or failing to do so. Plato pictured reason as a charioteer controlling unruly steeds, our emotions and instincts, in his dialogue the *Phaedrus,* a view stemming from his *dualism.* Aristotle envisioned more harmony between the soul and body in his theory of *hylemorphism,* a theory Aquinas was later to adopt and adapt to Christian purposes.

- *Dualism* (*dua:* "two") sees an opposition between the body and soul such that the body is an obstruction to the pursuit of truth and goodness.
  - *Hylemorphism* is the view that the body, made of matter (*hyle*) and the soul or form (*morphe*), the principle of organization, unite in the cooperative unity that is man.

When we reflect on what it is that makes us "humans," we can discern a ladder or hierarchy of functions. The highest part of the human is what Aristotle calls the *rational soul*, which combines *reason* and *free will* (this anticipates the Christian theory of man being made in the *image of God*). *Moral virtue* perfects our *will, passions, and appetites*; *intellectual virtue* perfects our *mind*. What is the will? We experience our will as the "executive" in command of our chosen actions. Our will chooses (let's say, to go to work) and then "executes" the choice (by getting up, driving the car, etc.). It "goes out" towards a good that is presented to it by the mind, and this is the meaning of will as a "rational appetite." In II.6, he defines moral virtue:

> ***Moral virtue*** is a characteristic (*hexis*) involving choice, which consists in observing the mean relative to us, a mean which is defined by a rational principle, such as a man of practical wisdom would determine it (II.6; 1106b36-1107a2).

The three parts of this definition are:
- Characteristic/Habit (*hexis*)
- Choice
- The "mean"

We know that virtue is a characteristic or firm disposition to act in a certain way, and not a *feeling*, *innate quality* or a *lucky event*, because happiness is none of these. Aristotle calls virtue a "habit" that is acquired through repetition and choice. Just as we become athletes through repeated practice, we become courageous or temperate through like actions. We *choose* to be virtuous—we don't become courageous by simply admiring or thinking about bravery. He calls choice a "deliberate desire for things in our own power" (III.4), focusing our attention on the fact that *virtue, like happiness, is a choice.*

When we desire and choose to live virtuous lives, we are casting our net over the unruly and unpredictable sea of human emotion and circumstance. Like the best strains in Christendom, Aristotle plunged the virtuous man into the fray, and did not keep him pure by isolation. He envisioned a wide array of moral virtues, corresponding to a wide array of contexts, such as the domain of physical pleasure, all manner of social relationships, the giving and receiving of money, facing danger, receiving honor, and so on (*NE* IV-VII). Cultivating a virtue means hitting the *mean* or point of excellence on a continuum between two vices, one of *excess* (too much of a certain feeling or action) and one of *defect* (too little). The "mean" of *courage* lies in between the vice of *rashness* (too much confidence in situations of danger) and the vice of *cowardice* (too little). The "mean" of *liberality* lies in between the vice of *prodigality* (giving away too much money) and that of *miserliness* (giving away too little). The list of moral virtues is found in Books IV-VI, and is expanded and directed towards Christian purposes in the moral theology of St. Thomas Aquinas.

There are *two measures* or standards by which we judge our moral action. First, there is the standard of the *man of practical wisdom*. Aristotle assumed there were competent familial and cultural authorities whose combination of experience and common sense provide us with models of virtuous living. By observing these competent moral authorities, we know how to react to situations in a virtuous way—with the right motive, in relation to the right persons, in the right way and time. They show us what temperance, courage, justice, honesty, friendliness, etc. are, by their actions. This is the *objective* side of virtue, virtue taken from the "outside." The *subjective* or "interior" side of virtue comes into play as well, however, since every person has a different threshold for goodness. Virtue is lived out in unique and often ambiguous moral situations, and manifests itself according to different accents in different epochs.

Aristotle's ethics were an outgrowth of aristocratic Athenian society, but today we would expand their scope. For instance, if the paradigm of courage is the soldier facing death, we *also* see its reflection in the child

38

battling leukemia, in the prophetic words of an unseasonable truth-teller in the media-driven culture of death, or, as Aquinas says, in the Christian martyr. St. Thomas grafted Aristotle's theory of moral virtue onto a robust theology of human beatitude that directed the soul towards God through the interplay of the "natural" virtues, the "theological" virtues and the "gifts of the Spirit," as we shall see in the next section.

Moral action is like a craft that requires experience, not a manual of external observances.

Unlike the excellences of character that we call *moral virtues*, **intellectual virtues** are perfections of our *mind*. We develop the virtues of *science, intuition* and *wisdom* (*NE* VI) when we seek truth purely for its own sake—this is what mathematicians, physicists and theologians do. Knowing how a quark relates to a photon or knowing the ways that angels communicate may not help us in the practical details of life, but it does illumine the passion and dynamism towards the fullness of being that characterizes us as humans. The human is the being who seeks the truth, says John Paul II (*Fides et Ratio* #28). We develop the virtues of *practical wisdom* and *art* when we use our mind in *doing the good* and *making something beautiful or useful*.

Most important for ethics is the virtue of *doing the good,* called *practical wisdom* (called *prudence* by Aquinas). The person who has "practical wisdom" knows what life is all about, and has a knack of giving practical advice on how to "live out" the virtues. He "deliberates well about what is good or bad for man" (VI.5), and navigates a path towards goodness that we can imitate. Despite the accessibility of the life of virtue for all, Aristotle's system carried elitist overtones. Ethics is seen as an application of justice in citizens of the Athenian *polis* or city-state (which excluded slaves and barbarians, among others), and his system was this-worldly, since it denied personal immortality. Where *rationality* alone is the chief feature of humanity, the capacity for love and *relationship* is not central, a view that could be corrected in light of contemporary trends in bioethics that negate the value of the helpless and marginalized.

- As a nonreligious ethic (not informed by revelation), Aristotle's theory does not value each person as sacred as made in the image of God, and thus, certain values are absent or contradicted, such as Christian humility.
- As an aristocratic ethic, Aristotle's theory prizes personal self-sufficiency instead of interdependence.

Discussion Questions:

1. How does Aristotle define "moral virtue" and "intellectual virtue," and why are these "perfections" of the individual the key components of happiness?

2. Do you agree with Aristotle's list of moral virtues, and would you add or subtract any?

Readings:

- *NE* I.13; II-VI

CHAPTER SIX
The Roles of Friendship and Pleasure

By nature, we like to enjoy life and like to do so in the company of others. In *NE* VIII and IX, Aristotle discusses the different types of friendship, culminating in the "virtuous friendship" that regards the friend as worthy of dignity, not just as a vehicle of pleasure or utility. Aristotle's theory anticipates the friendship with God that is Christian charity, for the friendship of virtue involves "self-transcendence." In this highest version of friendship, persons are mutually attracted by their love of goodness and truth that is something standing *beyond* the relationship. For the relationship gurus of today, Aristotle's view must sound strange—we are to love our friends, but we are to love the truth *more*.

Pleasure is also an integral part of happiness, since virtue would be impossible if it were entirely difficult. While some philosophers took the puritanical view that *all* pleasure is *bad* (*dualists* thought that the body was evil, and pleasures were basically physical), others thought that *all* pleasure was *good* (*hedonists* think that pleasure is the *chief* good in life, and that all we do derives from it). Aristotle took the *middle* view that *the good or evil of a certain pleasure depends on the activity involved that produces it*. The twisted pleasure that psychopaths feel is evil, because their actions are evil. The pleasure of rescuing a drowning man is a good pleasure, because the action is virtuous. *Pleasure is a byproduct of actions when they are performed well.* Further, there are *higher* and *lower* pleasures. The pleasure that accompanies the alleviation of hunger through eating is not as perfect as the pleasure of experiencing something as true, good or beautiful.

Aristotle thought that contemplation, although intermittent, was the most pleasurable activity, since it was directed at the highest object. (*One day in Thy courts is better than a thousand elsewhere!* – *Psalm* 84.10) The criteria for happiness introduced in *NE* I.7 were *finality* and *self-sufficiency.* These apply to contemplation, in that we need little in the way of external goods for this activity, and *by nature, man desires to know.* Fr. Joseph Owens explains the relation of *bodily* and *external goods*, and *moral virtue*, to *contemplation* in the following way: The nature of happiness is found first and foremost in the life of contemplation, and only *secondarily* in the lower goods, insofar as these "contribute to the free and abundant exercise of contemplation." Unlike the modern temperament that is constantly driven outwards in a rush towards accumulation, sensory experiences and distractions, the Greek mind follows a secure path leading into the heart of man, where it finds a luminous order and a victory over the chains of time.

Discussion Questions:

1. Do you agree with Aristotle's conclusions about friendship? Why is pleasure not as important as the activity that generates it?

2. Do you think that the goal of "contemplation" (as conceived by Aristotle) harmonizes with the pursuit of community through friendship? Do you think that Christianity offers a different view of friendship and contemplation?

Readings:

- *NE* VIII-IX; X.1-8

CHAPTER SEVEN
Aristotle and Christian Philosophy

In Aristotle's ethics we see the person as a cooperative unity of soul and body, as the possessor of habits directed towards the truth that can be known and loved. This is why *Fides et Ratio* calls for a return to classical philosophy in the retrieval of Christian wisdom (#55).

> John Paul II viewed classical philosophy as implicitly open to the supernatural (*Fides et Ratio* #75).

In this sense, Aristotle's *Ethics* shows the search for truth is not a specialized discipline, but is a search for a comprehensive vision of life's meaning (#30). Against the twin errors of the *denial* of reason (as in *scientism*) and *emotivism* (which spawned the errors of *fideism, relativism,* and *biblical fundamentalism*: #53), Aristotle's thought provides a refreshing return to the dignity of human reason. His emphasis on the objective and rational character of morality stands in stark contrast to the errors of false autonomy and radical subjectivism, which led to what Pope John Paul II called "the crisis of truth" in *Veritatis Splendor* (#32). Even the notion of conscience (not found in Aristotle) has its roots in the confident application of universal knowledge of the good to a particular case, not in an individualistic ethic which denies a common human nature. Finally, the shift of our gaze towards *transcendence*, possible only through the renewed vitality of reason, is a necessary condition of cultural survival.

Aristotle's theory of happiness laid the foundation for Aquinas's Christian ethics of beatitude, but it labored under the view that happiness is not eternally possessed. Aquinas thought Aristotle's *eudaimonism* represented an "imperfect" form of happiness procured independently of divine providence and cut short by bodily death. Several questions haunt the student of Aristotle.

Is moral virtue a part of the "contemplative life" or just a preparation for it? Is Aristotle's ethics *elitist*? One could not imagine Aristotle's "wise man" sitting in his study while his neighbor's house burned down, but neither could one imagine him joining the Missionaries of Charity!

Several aspects of Aristotle's thought, including his emphases on autonomy and the privileged status of the few gifted individuals who can contemplate divine reality, combine to *downplay* the important aspects of compassion and the dignity of persons. Aristotelian virtue would eventually be transformed by the light of Christian grace at the hands of Aquinas. How could virtue remain the same after a provident and personal God saw it fitting to enter human history and suffer? The grace that lightens (and makes possible) the human task of *being good* also makes us fully and completely human, while fitting us for the higher liberty of friendship with God.

Discussion Questions:

1. How does the thought of Aristotle complement Pope John Paul II's views on the nature and tasks of philosophy?

2. Do you agree that Aristotle's thought needed transformed and expanded by Christian virtue? Why?

Readings:

- *NE* X.7-8

—PART TWO—
St. Thomas Aquinas's Ethics of Beatitude

Francisco de Zurbarán 1598 - 1664
Apoteósis de Santo Tomás de Aquino / The Apotheosis of St Thomas Aquinas 1631

REFLECTION

"God's glory or brilliance is the principle
of every nature and form."
(St. Thomas Aquinas, *In 1 Romans*, lectio 7)

"Joy in the truth is the happy life."
(St. Augustine, *Confessions* 10.23)

In this section, we study St. Thomas Aquinas's approach to happiness and human destiny as they flow from the twin streams of revelation and reason, in light of John Paul II's encyclical on the harmony of faith and reason, "Fides et Ratio," and his encyclical on Christian morality, "Veritatis Splendor." Steeped in the arguments of Aristotle and the philosophers, on the one hand, and refreshed by the fountainhead of Scripture and the Church Fathers, on the other, St. Thomas fertilized sacred theology with a wisdom that harmonizes the ideal of living in a moral order with the longer views of eternity. His is a broad wisdom that houses the many walks of life by joining prudence with charity and discipline with love.

We introduce in this section several important aspects of Aquinas's theory of happiness as developed in one of his major works written for students of theology, his *Summa Theologiae*. John Paul II's 1998 encyclical *Fides et Ratio* strongly recommends the study of his work, naming Aquinas "the apostle of truth" (#44; referring to Paul VI's *Lumen Ecclesiae*).

Chapter One

Fides et Ratio and the
Summa Theologiae

John Paul builds upon Leo XIII's 1879 encyclical *Aeterni Patris*, which gave Aquinas special standing as the Church's preeminent guide in philosophy and theology. But as some have noted, it is with a different motive that John Paul takes up the banner of St. Thomas. While the end of the nineteenth century saw the papacy defending *faith* against *reason* (viz., closed rationalist systems proposed by science and social sciences at the time), the end of the twentieth century witnessed the Supreme Pontiff defending *reason* against *unreason*.

The present crisis of meaning in philosophy and in culture is lodged in the loss of confidence in the power of reason to reach the truth, and, as a consequence, a social conversation about values. But if the human being is defined as *one who seeks the truth* (*Fides et Ratio* #28), our human dignity is based on the call and capacity for the fullness of truth (#71) opened up by the wisdom of the Cross but disclosed in part in human nature and rationality. The errors to which closed systems of philosophy with their emphasis on autonomous or unaided reason have exposed humanity are detailed in the encyclical, and should serve as a beacon to warn men from shipwreck on their shoals.

Aquinas's theory of happiness, on the other hand, serves well in the rehabilitation of reason on its journey to the transcendent, and illustrates the power of reason's engagement with the mysteries of faith. In the second century, Tertullian asked, "What has Athens to do with Jerusalem?" and he proposed the triumph of revelation at the expense of human reason. Aquinas finds *his* answer in the intimate yearnings of the human heart that reach beyond even the passion of Athenian wisdom (#24, re *Acts* 17.22-27) to the friendship of God.

It is in this work that the pagan theory of happiness found in Aristotle's thought is taken up into the framework of Christian anthropology, where grace perfects and fulfills the basic capacities of human nature. The *Summa Theologiae* reflects Aquinas's favorable impression of Aristotle, whom he refers to simply as "the Philosopher." Aristotle's *Nicomachean Ethics* is extensively used in that work: Nearly one half of all the references to Aristotle in the *Summa* are to the *Ethics*, with Aristotle being used alongside Scripture and the Church Fathers as Aquinas's key authorities or sources.

> The brevity of this study necessarily limits our focus to some but *not all* of the key components in St. Thomas Aquinas's Christian theory of happiness. Important elements such as the development of "conscience," the precepts of "natural law," the precise nature of deliberative reasoning in moral choice, and the stimulating influence of grace in the moral life (through the theological virtues and "gifts") will be noted, but cannot be treated in the depth they deserve.

Aquinas stood at the forefront of a movement to utilize pagan sources such as Aristotle in the development of Christian theology, to "spoil the Egyptians" as it were, and was among the first generation able to absorb the *Nicomachean Ethics* through the Latin translation of Robert Grosseteste made available in 1246-47. In comparison with strictly philosophical works such as Aquinas's *Commentary on the "Nicomachean Ethics,"* the *Summa* shows Thomas subsuming the material from Aristotle into a Christian framework inspired by revelation. This approach stems from the necessity of following the "theological order" of the *Summa* that uses philosophy as a "handmaid" (*ancilla theologiae*) in the pursuit of truth. This path differs from that of unaided or purely human reason by starting with questions about God and His nature, then continuing with a descent (*exitus*) to questions about the created order, and finally returning (*reditus*) to God by way of salvation through Christ and the sacraments.

The return to God also occurs on the level of our human nature, which continues its trajectory towards God insofar as our free acts are governed by truth and ultimately by Providence. In *Veritatis Splendor* (#72), Pope John Paul II explains the interdependence of reason, freedom, and the eternal law: "The *morality of acts* is defined by the relationship of man's freedom with the authentic good. This good is established, as the eternal law, by Divine Wisdom which orders every being towards its end: this eternal law is known both by man's natural reason (hence it is 'natural law'), and—in an integral and perfect way—by God's supernatural Revelation (hence it is called 'divine law')." So, morally good action flows from freedom in conformity with our ultimate good, God, in whom we find our "full and perfect happiness."

Although we focus here on the *philosophical* elements of Aquinas's theory of happiness as found in the Second Part of the *Summa* (*ST* I-II and II-II), we must keep before us two facts: First, Aquinas chose to develop his theory within the underlying *theological* pattern of the *Summa,* between the First Part (*ST* I), which studies God, trinity, and creation, and the Third Part (*ST* III), which studies the incarnation and the sacraments. Second, man as a "moral" creature possesses both intellect and freedom of choice, and is thus a person made in the image of God. We can thus expect to find data from both revelation (theology) and reason (philosophy) woven together in his analysis of moral action, a unity reflective of the cooperation of grace and humanity in our pursuit of happiness. Morality for Aquinas is not a purely *human* project of character-formation or "soul-making" through our effort in the natural or "acquired" virtues any more than it is an isolated program of Catholic devotion, but is the richly personal process of fulfilling our highest potential and of sanctifying the world.

> The placement of Aristotle's thought within a Christian theological context in the *Summa* brings to prominence these two facts: First, earthly happiness is incomplete or fragmentary, a point Thomas even credits Aristotle with making. Second, "perfect" happiness is experienced only in the consummation of love and knowledge in the beatific vision in the afterlife.

As Fr. Joseph Owens points out, perfect beatitude is secured by the cooperation of divine providence and human choice, but is tasted in the life of Christian virtue here and now. Further, it is by the introduction of the Christian doctrines of creation and providence that Aquinas is able to transform Aristotle's this-worldly, elitist and achievement-driven concept of happiness into a theory that views human fulfillment as both service and gift, a life of "acquired" and "supernatural" virtue operating within the ambit of grace and open to each immortal soul.

Discussion Questions:

1. How does St. Thomas's "theological order" distinguish his approach to happiness from that of Aristotle, and how does Pope John Paul II's definition of man reflect that vision?

2. Do you think that we should seek happiness through drawing on both faith and philosophy? If so, what are the most important contributions of reason to this endeavor, and how should our minds be guided by faith?

Readings:

In addition to Pope John Paul II's encyclicals (*Fides et Ratio; Veritatis Splendor*), there are readings to accompany the chapters (Note: "*ST* I-II 5.1" = Aquinas's *Summa Theologiae*, First Part of the Second Part/Prima Secundae, Question 5, article 1).

- *ST* I-II, Prologue; *ST* I 103.5

CHAPTER TWO
Desire for an Ultimate End: Happiness

Aquinas's understanding of happiness, like Aristotle's, is teleological (i.e., ordered to an ultimate end), as the Prologue to the First Part of the Second Part (Prima Secundae) of the *Summa* states. Aquinas starts by analyzing the nature of an ultimate end in relation to human action. Elsewhere, he notes that the proper task of moral philosophy is to "consider human actions insofar as they are ordered to each other and to their end" (*Commentary on Nic. Eth.* lectio 1 #2). In order to assemble the elements of happiness in Aquinas, then, we need to study what the ultimate end is for him, and which human actions lead to it, all the while clearly defining the relationship of Aquinas's Christian theory of happiness with the pagan version found in the *Nicomachean Ethics*.

In *ST* I-II 1-3, we see St. Thomas introducing an element from the Christian authority St. Augustine, to clarify the nature of happiness. There are several differences between Aristotle's pagan conception of happiness and St. Thomas's Christianized version, influenced also by St. Augustine. What are these?

First, Aristotle focused on the proper feature of humans, viz., rationality, to determine the type of activity that constitutes our happiness, viz., contemplation. St. Augustine focused first on the *thing that is happiness itself—the "object"* of our highest activity, which is God, the "highest good" (*summum bonum*). St. Thomas accepts this priority of the "object" to the "activity" in his discussion of our final end, and thus shows his indebtedness to St. Augustine's treatise *On the Happy Life* (*De Beata Vita*). Along with his master St. Augustine, he states that although happiness belongs to the soul (and not the body), that which constitutes our happiness (the "object") is something *outside* the soul (I-II 2.7).

Second, Aristotle rejected Plato's "abstract Good" as useless to the practical, human project of morality (*NE* I.6), preferring the human ability to *think* to any transcendent *God*. St. Thomas introduced the topic of the freedom of the human will (I-II 1.2) so fond to St. Augustine, to make a move towards God in his argument. By invoking the idea of freedom, St. Thomas denied the ability of any created good to satisfy our thirst for happiness, proposing instead the "universal good" (I-II 2.8) that is God. The human mind and the human will are expansive powers directed towards infinite truth and goodness.

Third, because he lacked the idea of a personal, providential Creator, Aristotle's happy man could only *imitate* the gods from afar—we can achieve what these gods are but only in a lesser, self-enclosed way, some say. St. Thomas's happy Christian, on the other hand, *participates* in the inner life of God through the theological virtues and in the beatific vision.

> In his treatment of the relation of "happiness" and the "end of man" in *ST* I-II 1-3, St. Thomas synthesizes elements from Aristotle and St. Augustine. Although there has been much debate as to whether St. Thomas's theory of man is more "Aristotelian" or "Augustinian," it is clear that his treatise on happiness *uses* Aristotle's conception of the intrinsic and proper acts of things to construct an Augustinian conception of our final good as transcendent and personal, responding to our appetite for universal goodness. Aristotle's teleologically ordered human

nature reaches God through moving from a desire for particular goods to an explicit love of goodness and truth, and through responding in faith to God's invitation to communion with Him. The topic of happiness displays Aquinas's use of authorities in his *Summa:* the Scriptures, the Church Fathers, medieval theologians and ancient and Neo-Platonic philosophers. The three general kinds of authorities for Christian philosophy are: revelation, reason, and experience.

In the first section of the Second Part (*ST* I-II), Aquinas develops the general principles of Christian morality, identifying the final end of man as the vision of God. In the second part (*ST* II-II), Aquinas studies both the acquired (humanly developed) and the divinely "infused" virtues, including the key theological virtues of faith, hope and charity. The first five questions of *ST* I-II, however, are aimed at discovering the nature of happiness, the ultimate end of intelligent being. While the "appetite" for completion or perfection is found in all levels of life (vegetative, sensory and rational), a thing's final or ultimate end, he says, is that which marks a thing's perfection and fulfilling good (I-II 1.5).

Happiness is not the fulfillment of just *any* desire for *any* object, however, but is marked with an objectivity that also accompanies lower creatures' direction towards their more determined or fixed ends. Even those things that do not possess conceptual knowledge (animals, plants) nonetheless operate for the sake of the good, and in their own way have an appetite for the divine likeness through reaching their own perfection (*Summa Contra Gentiles* III 24).

Aquinas explains in the *Summa* that irrational beings can't direct themselves to their goals (trees growing, rabbits replicating) but are driven by instinct to a fixed end, like an arrow shot by an archer to its target

(I-II 1.2). Humans, on the other hand, move *themselves* to their exalted end of spiritual perfection through will and reason. We not only perceive our goals (e.g. health, knowledge, friendship), but also the means to reach these goals (exercise, books, visits). This self-directedness, which is a result of reflection, is made possible by the immaterial nature of the human intellect and its subordinate power, the will, or the "rational appetite."

Human beings perceive truth and desire goodness in a way different than animals, as is proven by our ability to resist the call of animal appetite, compare alternative courses of action, and analyze data scientifically. Aquinas speaks of an object of a power as that to which a power tends or is directed (I-II 2.8), and says that our mind having as its object the *universal true*, and the will as having the *universal good* as its object, pointing to the transcendent term or fulfillment of human nature.

> Every other creature (including the universe in its entirety), Aquinas explains, has goodness only "by participation" (they have partial, not full goodness), whereas the human being's intellectual powers (mind, will) reach out endlessly towards perfection, such that only God can satisfy our metaphysical "thirst" (*ST* I-II 2.8).

We can deliberate among particular goods, assessing them as means or steps towards an end (which, for example, will procure the good of knowledge: play or study?), and know particular and more general truths (as, for example, basic scientific maxims or laws are distinct from their applications). Regarding our search for *happiness,* certain means help us achieve certain ends, and these are all perceived under a further end, the general (if often implicit) *concept of the good (sub ratione boni).* We choose health (and the means towards it) because it appears good to us, and it is in fact also objectively good for us since it is a partial fulfillment of our nature as human beings.

Discussion Questions:

1. What ideas does St. Thomas adopt from Aristotle, and what ideas does he adopt from St. Augustine, in his picture of human fulfilment? Do you agree that happiness refers to something "beyond" our soul?

2. How do humans and animals differ in their relation to their ends, and how is this point significant for our search for happiness?

Readings:

- *ST* I-II, Prologue; *ST* I-II 1-3

Chapter Three
"Human Acts" and "Acts of Man"

Recalling our earlier section on Aristotle, we saw that happiness consists not in feelings or tendencies, but rather in *actions* that perfect the human person. Quoting St. Thomas (*ST* I-II 1.3), Pope John Paul II emphasizes the causal power of our human acts, which, by giving moral definition to our very person, determine our *"profound spiritual traits"*: "Human acts are moral acts because they express and determine the goodness or evil of the individual who performs them" (*Veritatis Splendor* #71). Aquinas also draws the distinction between human acts and acts of man. Human acts flow from reason and free will (I-II 1.3) and are relevant to morality, and so subject to moral evaluation as morally good or evil. Acts of man include actions which are involuntary (scratching one's head), or nonmoral (turning on a light), or otherwise seemingly irrelevant to our project of happiness.

A problem here emerges however, in realizing that some acts that flow from human freedom (playing the flute, for instance) do not appear to be subject to moral appraisal, yet they seem to be what Aquinas calls *human acts*. Let us take an example from medieval times:

> The intention to mirror and glorify divine transcendence through immensity of light was obvious in the creation of Bristol Cathedral Abbey in the twelfth century, revealing the intensely *human* act of its architect. But could the stonemasons' accomplishment of this technical feat by linking the internal pillars with horizontal bridges running across the arches, also be described as a "moral" act, since it uses mind and will?

For Aquinas, this is indeed a moral act, even though it is also a technical act, because the use of a certain power in particular circumstances can be morally evaluated (I-II 56.3). It is not the state of his tools or his expertise that qualifies the stonemason's cutting as morally good or bad; it is the disposition of his will in relation to the overarching good of his life. His act is *virtuous* if doing it makes him *good*. (Aquinas devoted much care to studying the various "criteria" involved in making an action morally good, including the act's end, its object, and circumstances.) How the act of cutting is situated with respect to his human destiny is the issue at hand.

Does it further the virtues that perfect him as a human being? Aquinas adopts Aristotle's division of virtue into "intellectual" and "moral" in I-II (58.3), such that virtue must perfect either the speculative or practical intellects (to be an intellectual virtue) or the appetites of the soul (to be a moral virtue). The stonemason uses the mind's practical virtues of art and prudence (studied below) in his act of building, and exercises several moral virtues as well.

Discussion Questions:

1. What does St. Thomas mean by saying that only "human acts" are moral acts, properly speaking, and why does it matter?

2. Do moral acts *flow from* our freedom and rationality, or *form* these powers, or *both*?

Readings:

- *ST* I-II 1.3; I-II 58.2-3

CHAPTER FOUR
Identifying Happiness

The difficult and important question is, of course, the issue of our *ultimate* end or destiny as humans. Is this end an activity of our *bodily senses*, of our *reason*, or of something *beyond* even our very souls? That we are directed towards complete fulfillment or happiness necessarily, or without choice, is a fact Aquinas takes for granted. We "naturally" seek or intend what we envision as fulfilling our lives. Everything is sought under the umbrella of the good (*sub ratione boni:* I-II 4.6). None of us would willingly and rationally seek our own unhappiness. Even suicide is a choice (albeit a bad one) for peace, not for nonexistence. The end (happiness) acts as a principle or starting point of action, in this case, for choice of particular goods (I-II 1.4-6).

Since happiness is the implicit motive for all of our actions, yet is in reality the very last thing to be attained, Aquinas often says that "what is first in intention is last in execution." Realizing that the drive for happiness steers all our actions and choices, we must nonetheless discover the true definition of happiness, or we shall be like ships without a rudder. To become happy then, we must reason *backwards* from this proper notion of happiness (what is intended), to discover the activities that will get us there, not unlike an architect who contracts out the work of building his masterpiece. The knot the philosopher must untie in this project is the process of distinguishing "true" from "apparent" happiness (evaluating varying ideas of what our *end* truly is), and of making proper deductions from this starting point (finding the right *means* to reach this end) (I-II 1.7).

ST I-II 2.1-4 excludes the external or worldly goods of wealth, honor, fame, and power, as candidates for happiness, since they all depend on a good beyond themselves. The bodily goods of health and survival are also excluded (2.5) because they do not comprise our total good nor do they order the human person to something beyond the self. (Happiness eludes the narcissist because we are made in the image of goodness and truth, not vice-versa!) *Pleasure* is rejected because it accompanies acts, and does not express their proper content or essence (2.6). There is no such thing as free-floating pleasure, but only pleasure of various types of acts (sensory, intellectual, volitional).

The *goods of the soul,* namely, reason and free choice as expressed in *culture,* seem closer to our final end, but these are also put aside in the recognition of the radical incompleteness of limited creaturely goods, no matter how noble (2.7-8). While we can call ourselves happy in exercising these functions (Aquinas's language of "use" in 2.7), our possession of these goods is only a share or "participation" in the fullness of the *universal* and *infinite* goodness and truth we desire as beings open to God (*capax Dei*).

What, then, corresponds to the human desire for infinite truth and goodness? Only the *divine good* of God's essence can "lull the will" (2.8) and so constitute our happiness. Here, Aquinas adopts Aristotle's statement that we are seeking the most perfect *activity* of our most perfect *power* with respect to the most perfect *object*: Not Aristotle's impersonal separate substances that steer the movement of the universe, nor the lofty good of contemplation itself, but the supremely personal, intelligible, and loveable object: God (3.5).

> Thus, our perfect happiness is to be found in the beatific vision, the act of contemplating and loving the divine essence, in which all the goods of the universe are contained and transcended. Aristotle's emphasis on the complex project of happiness gives way to St. Augustine's *summum bonum* (the highest good: God) who is the lover of the soul.

The happiness afforded by the use of our practical and speculative intellect on earth is called "imperfect" happiness, in contrast to the un-interrupted perfection of contemplation in the beatific vision (3.5; 3.8). The vision of God's essence alone satisfies our inquiry into the *causes* of things, into the *"what it is" that causes things to be* (3.8; cf. *ST* I 12.1).

Discussion Questions:

1. How does St. Thomas defend his view that only an infinite being (God) can satisfy the heart, and do you agree with his view? How would you defend this view to a modern pagan?

2. Do you agree that we need a "rear-view mirror" vision of happiness (that is, we must reason *from* a correct view of happiness *to* particular acts and choices in daily life) to be flourishing persons?

Readings:

• *ST* I-II 2-5

CHAPTER FIVE
Perfect and Imperfect Happiness

A key distinction is at work here between *perfect* happiness, which corresponds to our *supernatural* and heavenly *end*, and *imperfect* happiness, corresponding to fulfillment of our natural powers on earth (4.5). *Imperfect* happiness consists in our moral and contemplative acts and habits (the highest goods of the present life) rooted in the natural inclination to virtue and acquired by practice and study as outlined in Aristotle's *Nicomachean Ethics*.

This sort of happiness involves the requirements of Aristotle's *eudaimonia*, such as "external" and "bodily" goods as instruments for the work of moral and intellectual virtue, the "spiritual" goods (4.7). Insofar as it is based on the natural law, which is "universal" or common as inscribed in our rationality, our human happiness reflects the order of inclinations outlined by Aquinas (*ST* I-II 94.2) as reiterated by Pope John Paul II (*Veritatis Splendor* #51): "In order to perfect himself in his specific order, the person must do good and avoid evil, be concerned for the transmission and preservation of life, refine and develop the riches of the material world, cultivate social life, seek truth, practice good and contemplate beauty."

While dependent on human freedom and thought, this sort of happiness is nonetheless unachievable for some, and it is intermittent and subject to loss, being dependent on circumstance. It cannot be the ultimate end of human nature, since the will is ordered to *universal* and *infinite* goodness (2.8), whereas the goods of this earth are like refractions of a more perfect light, the perfect and sufficient good.

There has been much debate over the relation between the "natural desire" for happiness and its *supernatural* fulfillment in heaven. It is clear that Aquinas says there is *one* ultimate end (I-II 1.4-5), and yet human nature has its own finality and fulfillment in earthly contemplation. How can an end dictated by our nature be fulfilled in a supernatural order? This is a complex issue, but at least we can say that humans are by nature ordered to know the ultimate cause of all things as perfectly as possible. The supernatural vision of God goes beyond the earthly contemplation of God in His "effects" (creatures) to a vision of God in His own inner life. As one scholar put it,

> our ultimate natural end becomes, with the coming of the supernatural order, auxiliary or instrumental to our ultimate supernatural end—a change which, evidently, must have tremendous consequences for our natural humanity (A. Nichols, *Discovering Aquinas* [London: Darton, Longman & Todd, 2002] p. 95).

Elsewhere Aquinas writes that even the fulfillment of goods proper to our nature requires the initiative of *God*, supplying grace (see I-II 109.2). Experiencing the beatific vision involves the mind knowing God and the will delighting in this possession (5.2) by help of an elevating "form illuminating the mind" (called the *light of glory*)—by this light we are made like to God (I 12.5). The natural law, then, should be understood in continuity with the entirety of Providence's governance of the rational being. It is, as Pope John Paul states (*Veritatis Splendor* #40), following Aquinas, "the light of understanding infused in us by God, whereby we understand what must be done and what must be avoided." The "rightful autonomy" of practical reason is not an isolated individualism, for reason does not create its own values and moral norms; rather, these are received from the Creator (*Veritatis Splendor* #40).

> In the end, human beatitude is less the result of human virtuous effort than it is a response to God's special love for the rational creature, raising it above its natural condition "to have a part in divine goodness."
>
> (*ST* I-II 110.1)

Discussion Questions:

1. St. Thomas's Christian view of beatitude goes *beyond* earthly or "imperfect" happiness. What are the parts of Aristotle's theory on which St. Thomas draws, and in what ways does Christian happiness go beyond the pagan, Greek view?

2. How could the set of human "inclinations" (in the natural law) presented by St. Thomas and reiterated by Pope John Paul II be relevant both to a life of unaided human reason, and to the dynamic life of faith?

Readings:

- *ST* I-II 2.8; 3-5; I-II 94.2

CHAPTER SIX
The Passions and Friendship

Since the moral arena is one of *actions* and *emotions,* governing the passions is a large part of the moral task for Aquinas, as for Aristotle. Aquinas's study of the passions takes twenty-seven questions in the Prima Secundae, a fact which reveals their prominence for the study of virtue. As the Prologue indicates, this part of the *Summa* is devoted to the consideration of man as the image of God insofar as he is the principle and master of his acts through reason and free will. We have seen that reason has diverse activities that work together to achieve happiness. First, reason can pursue truth for its own sake, as in the case of the "intellectual" virtues. Second, reason works in a *practical* way in guiding the will, emotions, and appetites towards fit actions (cf.58.2-3; 64.1; I 81.3), as seen in the "moral" virtues. We can imagine the one power of reason sometimes fully concentrated in its theoretical contemplation of reality, and at other times spreading or extending itself outwards in the concrete circumstances of life, judging the measure of goodness of different actions (Aquinas said that the "true" *extends* to the "good" in his *Commentary on the Sentences* (I 27.2.1; cf. *ST* I 79.11).

There are different classes of emotions or passions. Some are only seated in the "rational" appetite or will, such as *love, joy* and *sorrow.* Others are acts of the "sensitive" appetite (an appetite is a natural inclination of a being towards its fulfillment—a "going out" towards perfection; see *ST* I 80.1). These latter involve the attainment of a real or apparent good, such as the passions of *delight, sadness, desire,* and *aversion, love* and *hatred* (emotions of the *concupiscible* appetite); or they refer to a good qualified by some difficulty in achievement, such as *hope* and *despair, courage* and *fear,* and *anger* (in the *irascible* appetite). Aquinas links these passions with the virtues responsible for either stimulating or restraining them, viz., temperance and fortitude/courage; seeing a close connection between passions and the physical body whose appearance and condition are often transformed by their influence.

While the passions may seem opposed to reason at first (this is the view Plato adopted, as seen in his image of the charioteer controlling the steeds in his dialogue the *Phaedrus*), they can "participate" in rationality by coming under its sway, and either help or hinder us to navigate the difficulties of life. They are neither bad (as the Stoics held) nor good in themselves (as "emotivists" claim, reducing all statements to emotional ones) then, but morally indifferent or neutral. It is not the mere *presence* of an emotion but what we *do* with it that counts, morally.

When experienced voluntarily, passions take their moral quality from their relationship to reason (I-II 24). Involuntary emotions can *become* voluntary by the will's commanding them (a feeling of hope in trials, for instance) or resisting them (to refuse to consent to their prompting when it is against reason, as in the case of unjustified anger). Rationally regulated passions are at work in the movement *towards* moral virtue (the process of gaining the habit of virtue), as a sign of virtue's *stability* (proper emotions are a sign of the presence of virtue), and as aids in spiritual *progress* (in prompting the virtues directed to God's service).

The study of the passions in Aquinas reveals a startling contrast with the privileged role they are granted in contemporary culture, as the untamed gods of the sovereign individual. Passions are an integral part of our moral story, but are not its main message or even syntax, which ordering role is given to reason. Under reason's guidance, however, they do express the varying rhythm and changing intensity of a well-ordered life.

> The foundation of all the passions is *love* (*amor*), which is the source of a movement directed towards a desired object or end, and as such, is included in all kinds of love: *dilection (dilectio)*, which involves choice; *friendship* (*amicitia*); and *charity* (*caritas*), which is the love of friendship between man and God, and is the most proper and perfect form of love (*ST* I-II 26.1-3).

In *amor,* the thing loved is perceived as an apt fulfillment of a power, and in man, is presented to the will under the aspect of goodness, which encompasses the "good" or virtuous, the "pleasant" and the "useful" (*ST* I 5.6). Unlike *knowledge*, which assimilates or takes in information, *love* takes a good as presented to the will by the mind, and as appetitive, goes out towards an object in order to possess and enjoy it (I-II 26.2). In the case of irrational creatures, the appetite of love is a kind of "weight" towards the thing's natural fulfillment, but in the case of man, love also exists at a higher level, in which one can distinguish the love of a *person* from the love of the *good* one wills for him. The "love of *concupiscence*" is the love of a *good* for another, while the "love of *friendship*" entails the love of the person for his own sake (26.4). These need not stand in opposition, since the wishing of good to another that is love involves both loving a person *and* his good.

71

Discussion Questions:

1. How does St. Thomas differ from Plato's view of the emotions, on the one hand, and the Stoics' view, on the other? Do you agree with St. Thomas?

2. How does St. Thomas's view of the emotions (especially, "love") differ from the notion of love in our culture today?

Readings:

* *ST* I 80-82; I 5.6; I-II 22-46

Chapter Seven

Friendship with God

Following Aristotle, Aquinas notes that friendship involves benevolence, reciprocation and a shared good (II-II 23.1). Departing from him, he notes that friendship with God is possible thanks to the shared form that is God's own beatitude, given gratuitously to men, making them "equals" not through merit but by *fiat*. Whereas for Aristotle, friendship is an *instrumental means* for earthly happiness, an aristocratic exchange among equals, for Aquinas, friendship is possible with God, whose unmerited love is displayed in the acts of creation, the Incarnation, and redemption.

Loving friendship with God is not merely a passion but a *theological virtue* or *habit* (fixed disposition) called charity (*caritas*), a divinely infused virtue impossible on the plane of natural, acquired virtues developed by Aristotle. We neither initiate nor merit being friends with God, for like grace itself, charity is impossible without God's initiative. He desires something good for us (namely, His very own eternal happiness) in the union of love, before we respond with a love for God in Himself (beyond the gifts He confers).

> The sixth century Syrian theologian Dionysius the Areopagite ("Pseudo-Dionysius") contributed this idea of love as a "unitive force" to Aquinas's analysis of *caritas*, an idea that tempers the *intellectual* character of the beatific vision with the affective union of *love*.

A final point to note here regards the final end of man, the beatific vision. Unlike faith and hope (the other "theological" virtues), charity is not provisional, and will not fade away but becomes perfect in the beatific vision. Nonetheless, we attain this union with God by an act of the *intellect* in its speculative role, with our will's act of love only accompanying this vision (I-II 3.3-4). This priority of cognition to appetite is not a question of the mind's greater "nobility," but is a question of the interplay of the intellect and will. Nothing is loved unless it is first known, at least to some extent (I-II 3.4 ad 4). In describing the supernatural end of man, philosophy bumps up against the limits of language; for although both our mind and will enjoy the beatific vision in the act of contemplation, neither can fully grasp its infinite, divine object of God, now experienced directly, not just through His created effects.

Some mystics have referred to the experience of prayer as a most "busy rest," which hints at the kind of dialectic between love and knowledge encountered in the face of infinite mystery in this final state.

Discussion Questions:

1. What are the ways in which St. Thomas's view of friendship differs from that of Aristotle, and which view do you appreciate more?

2. How is the theological virtue of charity distinct from both the emotion of love and from our reason, and yet is related to both?

Readings:

- *ST* II-II 23-27; I-II 26-28; *On Charity* IX-XI

CHAPTER EIGHT
The Moral, Intellectual, and Theological Virtues

Aquinas's theory of natural or acquired (vs. supernatural or infused) virtues reveals dependence on Aristotle's anthropology of powers and perfections, and on the distinction of theoretical and practical knowledge. He adapts Aristotle's definition of virtue as a perfection of a human power that enables a person to act well (I-II 55.4, e.g.): Virtues are habits that help us to attain our end. Three of the five *intellectual* virtues engage reason in its activity of pursuing *truth for its own sake* (*understanding, science,* and *wisdom*), and two engage reason in its guiding and directive function of the emotions, appetites and body with an end to *action* (*practical wisdom or "prudence," and art*). The full array of naturally acquired (vs. supernaturally infused) *moral* virtues perfect our appetites and emotions, and puts "conceptual meat" as it were, on the bones of the virtues which condition our *entire* moral life, viz., the *cardinal virtues* of *prudence, courage, temperance,* and *justice*. In *ST* II-II, for instance, *chastity, abstinence,* and *sobriety* are some "parts" of *temperance,* while *confidence, patience,* and *perseverance* are some "parts" of *fortitude* (courage), *religion* and *filial piety* are "parts" of *justice,* and so on.

The virtue of "prudence" bridges the moral and intellectual virtues and is necessary for any of the moral virtues to operate, Aquinas writes. It is a perfection of the "practical" mind (which, we recall, applies knowledge to *doing* [prudence] or *making* [art]) and ensures correct judgment about what is to be done to secure our overall good (the *end*) and guides particular moral actions to their *mean*. In this way, prudence directs not only the moral virtues by applying them to situations here and now, but directs our exercise of the intellectual virtues as well (prudence is absent or faulty in the case of the scientist experimenting on fetuses, since his knowledge is misdirected).

Prudence involves good *deliberation* about the relation of means to ends ("learning" as a means to "knowledge" as part of our happiness, e.g.), good *application of moral precepts* (such as those found in natural law—the precepts are in I-II 94.2) and *judgments* about present action to be taken. It is neither prudishness nor cunning nor cleverness, because its end is true action alone, the real and not the apparent good for man. As one scholar expressed it, prudence is "the developed disposition to deliberate well, to decide well and to execute actions well" (B. Davies, *The Thought of Thomas Aquinas* [Oxford: Clarendon Press, 1992] p. 242).

Thomas distinguishes the *acquired* or *human* intellectual and moral virtues from the *infused theological* virtues of faith, hope, and charity, by means of different "rules" or measures and by distinct "objects." *Acquired* virtue takes *human reason* as its measure, since this sort of virtue seeks what fulfills human nature as considered by reason alone (without revelation). The *infused* theological virtues take *God* as their measure, for in their very definition, they relate us to God directly. Because there can never be too much faith, hope, or love of God, these virtues do not observe the "mean" of the acquired moral virtues, and when subject to the influence of grace, even the moral acquired virtues lose their observance of the mean. While "temperance" meant moderation in bodily appetites for Aristotle, it can involve extremes of fasting, bodily virginity, and asceticism under the impetus of grace.

To summarize, what are some of the key *differences* between Aristotle's pagan notion of happiness and St. Thomas's Christian version?

1. Our final end: For Aristotle, our final end is the activity of virtue with the complexity of human goods as their condition or support. By our contemplation, we *imitate* the gods' blessedness. For Aquinas, our final end is the "highest good" (*summum bonum*) that is God alone, Who calls us to *participate* in His own beatitude. St. Thomas speaks of the distinction between "imperfect" and "perfect" happiness, corresponding to the measure of happiness we can have in this world or in the next.

2. Reaching our final end: For Aristotle, we reach the end of contemplation by a combination of human effort and luck. For Aquinas, it is the emphasis on God's initiative through grace that makes the human effort of virtue possible, and specifies our end to be the "vision of God." We are naturally open to the vision of God and are supernaturally elevated to reach this end.

3. The status of moral virtue: For Aristotle, the moral virtues appear to be instrumental to happiness, but not constitutive of it. For Aquinas, they are intrinsic to happiness, since the formation of the human person happens through, and not in spite of, the tragedies of life. In his biblical commentaries, Aquinas reveals the paradoxical connection between suffering and the attainment of peace and happiness even in this life.

The "radicalization" of the moral life within the Christian realm does not compromise Aquinas's belief in the natural nobility of acquired virtue. However, it does remind us that acquired moral virtue is virtue in a *qualified* sense, because it orders us to purely *human* flourishing, not to our ultimate end of union with God (I-II 65.2).

> Like a sea admiral leading his fleet to the place of battle but then leaving the captains to their own judgments of attack, knowing their pledge to honor and valor will outweigh their individual interest (Admiral Nelson at the Battle of Trafalgar), so God draws the just soul into moral action, confident that its natural powers will obey the inner promptings of grace, viz., the theological virtues and gifts.

Thus, the topic of virtue highlights the limits of philosophy and the paradox of the human condition: To know and love God is the ultimate end of human nature (I-II 1.8); but we can neither intend nor achieve our end apart from grace (I-II 109.2). To solve this paradox through philosophy alone would be to mount stairs eroded by the tread of countless feet over the centuries with only the light of a sputtering candle — a task surely beyond the limits of this chapter.

Discussion Questions:

1. Explain how "natural" and "acquired" and "supernatural" and "infused" virtues contribute to our happiness, both in this life and the next.

2. How does the Christian life represent a "radicalization" of virtue? Can you give examples of this intensification of moral goodness that occurs under the influence of faith?

Readings:

- *ST* I-II 49-65; 68

—Part Three—
Pieper on Wisdom and Contemplation

Cloister Garth of St. Joseph's Abbey, Spencer, MA

Reflection

"He truly receives the Goodness of reality as a whole
only when he accepts it as pure gift."
(Josef Pieper, *In Tune with the World: A Theory of Festivity*)

"I say to you: Make perfect your will.
I say: take no thought of the harvest,
But only of proper sowing."
(T.S. Eliot, *Choruses from 'The Rock'*)

In this section, we examine Josef Pieper's work "Leisure: The Basis of Culture," and continue our reflection on Pope John Paul II's encyclicals "Fides et Ratio" and "Veritatis Splendor." These works combine to show that the imprisonment of human reason, either in the world of pure utility or in the court of its own judgment, presents impassable obstacles to the soul on its way to beatitude. A main concern of Pieper is the way in which the Christian philosopher, going about his Father's business, invests the everyday world with a sense of the sacred and of celebration. The "symphony of truth" (cf. Pope John Paul II, "Fidei Depositum") that uses the instruments of faith and reason together in a melodic structure that is the Catholic faith in its fullness, is the focus of "Fides et Ratio."

Josef Pieper's book *Leisure: The Basis of Culture* (1952) presents a thesis not unlike John Paul II's *Fides et Ratio* in that human dignity is said to rest on our search for the truth. The human being is defined as *the one who seeks the truth* (*Fides et Ratio* #28), as one who is capable of seeing *what is* and the *whole* of what is (*capax universi*). Pieper learned from Aristotle that the soul is somehow capable of "becoming" all things through knowledge, while St. Thomas and St. Augustine taught him that this vision of reality is consummated in the vision of God, in whom all things are known and loved.

In this section, we will trace some highlights of Pieper's argument that culture is grounded in a proper concept of leisure, and that leisure is guaranteed and expressed in the free transcendent acts of man, including the activity of philosophy, and through a connection with the transcendent, made possible through worship. We will see how Pieper's ideas anticipate the thought of John Paul II on the relationship between faith and reason; and we will contrast Pieper's theory to perspectives on human dignity found in various modern philosophies that have spawned our present cultural milieu.

CHAPTER ONE
Culture and the Philosopher's Vocation

In the first part of his book, Pieper discusses the original sense of "leisure" that is the basis of Western culture, and contrasts it to the more modern sense of "work" that destroys its very essence. While *Fides et Ratio* traced the decline of an earlier Christian metaphysical and moral vision of reality to a crisis of "rationalism" and eventually to modern nihilism and the postmodern denial of objective values and truth, Pieper focuses on the debasement of intellectual activity as a kind of socially useful "work" by totalitarian regimes (and by extension, any society that restricts the definition of persons to their material conditions).

> The common deficiency studied by both John Paul II and Pieper lies in two failures: The first is the inability to see human nature and creation as a divine "gift" that inspires the response of gratitude, fidelity, and celebration. The second is the failure to incarnate this kind of response within a culture that can guarantee our human freedom and dignity.

Since human beings are both children and parents of the culture in which they are immersed (*Fides et Ratio* #71), the challenge of the Christian philosopher is not to create an abstract system and impose it blindly on the raw material of culture. Rather, it is to make explicit the drive for the absolute present in every soul, by tracing it to its cause and source (God), thereby forming the vocabulary for a response that expresses our place in the cosmos and our unique dignity. This is the way Pope John Paul II links the notions of philosophy and culture:

> In reaffirming the truth of faith, we can both restore to our contemporaries a genuine trust in their capacity to know and challenge philosophy to recover and develop its own full dignity.... philosophy has the great responsibility of forming thought and culture; and now it must strive resolutely to recover its original vocation.... (*Fides et Ratio* #6).

John Paul insists that the Church has no one philosophy of her own (#49), since adoption of one philosophical system could hinder reason's progress towards the horizon of truth, and in effect limit the autonomy (and territory) of "philosophy." Nonetheless, *Fides et Ratio* continues the tradition of *Aeterni Patris* (1879) in recommending the guidance of St. Thomas Aquinas as the paradigmatic realist whose metaphysical vision serves as a good instrument to reclaim the ground lost by flirtations with the counterfeits of subjectivism, relativism and nihilism.

Pieper's thought about leisure springs from the rich soil of Aquinas's metaphysics, and the spirit of Pieper's survey of philosophical views of "work" resonates with Pope John Paul II's advice that scientists should retain the "sapiential horizon" in their search for truth, such that the values indelible to the human person are upheld (#106).

Philosophy has its own starting point, methods, and goals, for it is an autonomous discipline; but its conclusions can endanger the human dignity it seeks to promote, if it is pursued without reference to the transcendent. Anchored only to itself, it remains inert and unable to sail into the boundless ocean of truth (cf. *Fides et Ratio* #23); breaking free of the wisdom of the Cross, it falls under the heavier load of its own frame.

Discussion Questions:

1. What is the main challenge for the Christian philosopher, according to Pope John Paul II?

2. Why did Pieper think that totalitarian regimes lacked a proper sense of the philosopher's contribution to culture?

Readings:

In addition to Pope John Paul II's encyclicals (*Fides et Ratio; Veritatis Splendor*), there are readings to accompany the chapters (Note:*Leisure,* Part I = *Leisure: The Basis of Culture,* Part I; "*PA,* Part I" = *The Philosophical Act,* Part I)

- *Leisure,* Part I, II, IV

CHAPTER TWO
Work and Knowledge

In Parts Two through Four of *Leisure: The Basis of Culture*, Pieper contrasts the Greek and medieval ideas of leisure with the more modern sense of it as "idleness," a view ironically emerging through modernity's idolization of efficiency and "work." We have inherited this erroneous idea of leisure, Pieper writes, from various philosophies that either denied the mind's essential contact with external reality (Kant) or reduced its function to that of practical deliberation to fulfill material needs (Marx). Both positions restricted the proper activity of the speculative intellect and so cut off the possibility of contemplation and the spiritual interiority on which leisure depends. In effect, this led to the marginalization of philosophy from public discourse and to the emptiness of a culture without spiritual nourishment, a society of the ephemeral where "the possibility of discovering the real meaning of life is cast into doubt," so that many merely "stumble through life to the very edge of the abyss without knowing where they are going" (*Fides et Ratio* #6).

In Part One, Pieper introduces Aristotle's distinction of the servile and liberal arts in order to connect true leisure with the *artes liberales,* and to show how we have lost his sense of the term. Expanding on Pieper, we note that for Aristotle, the *liberal* arts (practiced by "freemen") are simply those activities that concern immaterial realities, the activities that "free" men from matter. Here he is not disqualifying the "fine arts" (such as music) but rather saying that their objects are not produced for gain or utility but rather enjoyed for their *own sakes* (literature, arts, philosophy, etc.). They are not destroyed by use (as a pie disappears when eaten) but can exist in many minds simultaneously (as a symphony is enjoyed by an audience). These goods as *ends* and not mere *means* draw us into contemplation, in contrast with the *servile* arts, material skills necessary to produce the necessities of life (e.g. shoemaking, building, medicine; here, "good" is taken merely as a means, or "utility").

Pieper contrasts the modern notion of "work" with the Greek idea of leisure as found in the liberal arts, noting the identification of a "person" with his "work" that has emerged in the West. Although Pieper is referring to the totalitarian regimes of Nazi Germany and communism, much of his analysis rings true in our day. Pieper proposes a return to a Christian philosophical conception of the human person as a corrective to the great "subterranean changes" wrought in our scale of values.

In Part Two, the genealogy of the idea of *intellectual work* is studied, in contrast to the Christian medieval affirmation of *contemplation* as the highest achievement of the soul. Immanuel Kant (1724-1804) limits human knowledge to the "work" of discursive activity (relating propositions, deducing conclusions etc.), denying the contemplative receptivity that grasps the things in themselves. The dynamism of the human intellect and its structures which determine the content of knowledge, are the concern of the philosopher, Pieper writes, and the merit of an act of philosophizing corresponds to the level of toil and pain it involves.

Certainly this picture of philosophy matches the image of Kant we have inherited: a punctual, plodding man, by whose walks one could set one's watch, who preferred to theorize about God in his study than to worship Him in church. Regarding Kant's claims on the limits of the human mind, Pieper would agree with the great Christian thinker G.K.Chesterton, that

> "to draw out the soul of things with a syllogism is as impossible as to draw out Leviathan with a hook."
>
> (G.K. Chesterton, *The Defendant* [1901])

Indeed, Kant's denial of the transparency of the world to the human mind is echoed in his moral and religious views, where the *moral act* becomes the work of *duty*, and the truths of immortality and God become mere "postulates" or *hypotheses* necessary for the reasonableness of life but still tragically opaque to our minds. The "three themes" noted by Pieper in this regard are important. Implicit in his book is the idea that every human being is a philosopher in the sense that every soul is, in essence, a lover of wisdom (*philo-sophia*) as open to all that is (*capax universi*). And the demotion of this humanizing characteristic that transforms the pilgrim of light into a mere *intellectual laborer/worker* stems from three beliefs:

- "knowledge" is not contemplative but is reduced to the active labor of *discursive* thought (in science, logic, and so on)
- "effort" and toil are the criteria of truth (and moral goodness)
- philosophy and the liberal arts exist only as "social services" and not in their own right

Discussion Questions:

1. How does the true idea of "leisure" differ from mere "idleness," and how has modern philosophy contributed to the current misconception of leisure?

2. Why has the modern world lost sight of "contemplation" and what is the modern (and mistaken) notion of philosophy? Do you think that the modern confusion about the nature of philosophy affects our daily lives? How?

Readings:

- *Leisure*, Part II-IV

CHAPTER THREE
Contemplation and the
"Philosophical Act"

Unlike Kant, Aquinas sees a cohesiveness or correspondence of the external world and the human mind. The human mind is able to receive knowledge and know things in their actual existence, not just syllogize and argue as in science, since both the world and the mind are providential *gifts*. It is their origin in the divine that guarantees the world's presence to our mind and our mind's ability to grasp that presence, Aquinas notes, quoting St. Augustine:

> "If we both see that what you say is true, and if we both see that what I say is true, then where do we see this, I pray? Neither do I see it in you, nor do you see it in me: but we both see it in the unchangeable truth which is above our minds."
>
> (*ST* I 84.5, quoting *Confessions* XII.xxv.35)

Behind the talk of the "intuitive" nature of contemplation in Pieper's book is a theory of knowledge (see Aquinas's *ST* I 79-88) that involves the "*active intellect,*" that which makes the forms of sensory things (e.g. "man") actually intelligible through "abstracting" them from their material conditions (the particularities of "John"), so that they can be "received" in the "*passive intellect.*" This activity is involved in *simple apprehen-*

sion by which a nature is known; there are also the activities of *existential judgment* (knowing the thing actually exists), *propositional judgment* (mind comparing concepts of *subject* and *predicate* in a proposition), *science* (deduction of propositions and conclusions; intellectual knowledge by means of causes), and eventually, the *contemplation of God and His effects in relation to Him* (which is either the "natural" science of first philosophy or "natural theology," or is the supernaturally infused virtue of "wisdom" by which the soul affectively experiences God). There are various types of "contemplation" in Aquinas; and Pieper stresses the value of contemplation of the *philosopher* in *The Philosophical Act,* which follows *Leisure: The Basis of Culture.* Here is a brief summary of Aquinas's use of the term:

> *Contemplatio* is a term used analogously by Thomas to refer to three levels of intellectual vision: natural, revealed contemplation ("acquired" contemplation), and supernatural or "mystical" contemplation. In all cases, contemplation refers to divine truth and its related effects, and is the work of the speculative intellect. Natural contemplation is the work of the philosophers, and ascends from creatures to grasp metaphysical truths about God. Revealed contemplation is the fruit of theological study, and attains God in Himself from revealed principles, but through the imperfect medium of faith. Mystical contemplation, the preserve of those sanctified souls infused with charity, also attains God's inner life, but through a supernatural mode.... Finally, the beatific vision, or the science of the blessed, is the knowledge of God through His own essence.
>
> (Heather McAdam Erb, *"Pati Divina: Mystical Union in Aquinas,"* in ed. A. Ramos, *Faith, Scholarship and Culture in The 21ˢᵗ Century* [Washington D.C.: CUA Press, 2002, pp. 79-80])

Pieper stresses the passivity, silence and tranquility of contemplation throughout his book, which lends leisure its "receptive attitude of mind." In chapters nine and ten of another work by Pieper, *Happiness and Contemplation*, he describes further his usage of *contemplation*. There he says contemplation is a "silent perception of reality" attained through "intuition" (the knowledge of what is actually present, not the deduction of conclusions) and accompanied by wonder or amazement.

How does this square with Pieper's discussion of contemplation in *The Philosophical Act*? In the latter, contemplation involves the silence of letting the mind rest its intuitive gaze on an object that is loved, which involves a sort of *ecstasy* or stepping outside of the "workaday world" of routine and utility (*Philosophical Act*, Pt. I; cf. *Leisure* Part V).

The element of wonder or amazement characterizes the philosophical act as distinctively "human" in that the object (the world as a totality) we lovingly intuit *exceeds our comprehension*. The relation of the "philosophical act" with the ideas of *totality* and *mystery* will be detailed below.

Discussion Questions:

1. What are the types of "contemplation" and how do they differ from scientific experiments?

2. Do you agree that contemplation involves both a "stepping out" of our "workaday world," yet also involves an appreciation of the ordinary? How?

Readings:

• *Leisure*, Part III-V; *PA* Part I

CHAPTER FOUR
Worship, Leisure and "Transcendent Activities"

We have said that Pieper links the notions of *culture, leisure, philosophy,* and *worship*: *leisure,* the basis of *culture,* is guaranteed only by the authentic practice of transcendent activities such as *philosophy*, which in turn are grounded in *divine worship.* Any reflective person can see the ways in which an aberrant notion of leisure, taken from the view that reduces humans to mere work units, ruins culture.

> The despair in our culture of distractions is evidence of the absence of interior peace and silence. As Augustine wrote in his *Confessions*, "My heart is restless until it rests in Thee."

A society where experiences are hoarded and persons seen as commodities for our assimilation does not lend itself to the free and joyful affirmation of the universe in the "festival." And yet it is this core of leisure, found in the real wealth of sacrifice and sacrament, that people desire in their search for a "way." Time and space that is set aside for worship alone is not wasted, but is non-useful in the ordinary mechanistic sense of serving a material need. The sense of reverence for *being* ("why is there something rather than nothing?") that is at the heart of worship is linked to the *philosophical act* in that both prayer and philosophy replace our "workaday" vision of things with a renewed *wonder* stemming from an experience of the mysterious nature of the universe.

French writer Charles Péguy linked the ideas of work, philosophical wonder, worship, and gratitude in his description of the work of the atelier/craftsman:

> We all know the value of work. We have all seen care carried to perfection, present in the whole, just as in the most intricate of details. We have known the piety of this "work well done"....
> It was necessary for the leg of a chair to be well made. It was not something to be done well for the sake of wages....It was necessary to do it well for its own sake, in itself, by itself, in its very being....
>
> This is the highest principle underlying the building of the great cathedrals....Everything was constant ceremony....the atelier was an extension of domestic ceremonial...The rhythm of hearth and handicraft were as one ceremonial from the first light of day....Everything tended to raise up the heart and mind, everything was a day long prayer, sleeping and waking, work and brief rest, the bed and the table, the soup and the meat, the house and the garden, the open door and the street, the farm-yard and the threshold of the home....And as a consequence, the splendid, affiliated and derived sentiments, the respect for the elderly, for parents, for the family....
>
> (Charles Péguy, *L'Argent*, tr. passage in Federico Suarez, *Joseph of Nazareth* [New York: Scepter Publishers, 2004], pp. 188-189)

The wisdom and immediacy of this incarnational reverie becomes even more apparent when juxtaposed with antichristian philosophies that completely sever the connection between mind and reality by making knowledge either an intoxicating "will to power" and revolt against community (Nietzsche), a hopeless project of privileging and oppression that needs "unmasked" or deconstructed (Derrida), or an illusory "metanarrative" purporting to disclose comprehensive, ultimate meaning but deceiving all (Lyotard, Rorty).

Pope John Paul II's analysis of the decline from truth into moral anarchy is an incisive expression of the disorder that this confusion unleashes. He explains the effects of sidelining objective truth from the moral realm. When truth is exiled, man's morality is said to flow from the "supreme tribunal" of his own moral judgment, distorting conscience as an act of intellect, and leading, in the end, to the "denial of the very idea of human nature" (*Veritatis Splendor* #32).

Péguy would agree with Pope John Paul II's assessment, as would the romantic realist Pieper. The poet might muse that these anti-contemplatives write as if they had never been young, never walked in the woods alone, or lingered outside the window of their beloved.

Pieper draws a connection (*Philosophical Act,* Part I) between worship and other incommensurable (mutually irreducible) activities that cannot be reduced to material gain, namely, *philosophy, the arts*, and *moments of existential shock* (moments of proximity to love or death, which reveal our radical contingence and dependence). All of these activities displace us by two means: a) they dislodge our ordinary, utilitarian attitude and replace it with a wonder at the beauty of the cosmos, the "whole" (what Pieper calls "piercing the canopy" of the workaday bourgeois world) and b) in their true form, they are characterized by a receptivity and gratitude that defines humanity as responsive to the divine gift of being. The freedom and generosity of this response mirrors the goodness of God Himself, who creates not out of necessity but out of the "self-diffusive" nature of His own goodness. The very quality of gratitude that is foreign to contemporary culture is closely related to both humility and joy. Gratitude rejoices in what is, and is humble in the knowledge of its dependence. One philosopher has expressed the connection between the gratitude of the philosopher and the artist:

The humility of Bach, the humility of Mozart, each so different (the former gives grace with unequaled genius, the latter, we might say, is grace itself) but both overwhelming in their happy gratitude, their true simplicity, their almost superhuman power; even in anguish and suffering, they have a serenity to them that stems from the knowledge of being an effect and not a cause....
(A. Comte-Sponville, *A Small Treatise on the Great Virtues* tr. C. Temerson [New York: Henry Holt, 2002], p. 136)

Gratitude is the property of both faith and philosophy. As love, it is the joy of response to one who inspires it, "a joy," Spinoza said, "accompanied by the idea of its cause."
(Spinoza, *The Ethics* III def. 6 of the emotions)

> **Ecstasy.** *etymology: ex-stasis (Gk) :* to "stand outside" oneself. The Greek cult of Dionysius had the aim of *extasis*—anything from "taking you outside of yourself" to a profound alteration of personality (E. R. Dodds, *The Greeks and the Irrational* [Berkeley, CA: University of California Press, 1951], p. 77). Philosophically, it is the wonder of contemplating being or beauty as echoed in Plato's *Symposium* and Plotinus' *Enneads* (III.8; VI.9; I.6).

Our moments of conscious gratitude are also expressions of Christian freedom acquired in love, which, as Pope John Paul II emphasizes, is manifested in the "gift of self." Not to be identified with volunteerism or mere human kindness, Christian love soars beyond philosophical insight, and has its source in grace. This love is lived on the "highroad" of the "contemplation of Jesus Crucified," the "never-ending source from which the Church draws unceasingly in order to live in freedom" (*Veritatis Splendor* #87).

Discussion Questions:

1. In what ways has a wrongheaded idea of "leisure" affected our Western culture? What is Pieper's remedy for this situation? Do you agree?

2. How would Pope John Paul II agree with Pieper's diagnosis of modernity's incapacity for true leisure and contemplation? Does one need gratitude to be a good philosopher, and if so, why? How is gratitude linked to love and humility?

Readings:

- *Leisure*, Part V; *PA* Parts I-II

Chapter Five
World, Spirit and "Inwardness"

In *The Philosophical Act*, Parts Two and Three, Pieper explains both the positive and negative aspects of the *philosophical act*. On the positive side, to "philosophize" takes man beyond the effort of adapting himself to his immediate physical environment (sphere of material needs) into the *world* (range or field of relationships that he has). On the negative side, philosophy cannot fully answer the questions about God, the soul, and the world that it poses, and must turn to revelation for its final fulfillment. Even the finite reality of a human soul is, in the end, a mystery only partially accessible to rational experience, yet is illumined in its origin, present condition, and destiny by the data of faith.

"Problem" vs. "Mystery":

French Christian existentialist Gabriel Marcel distinguished the *problem* we control and solve from the *mystery* in which we participate:

"A *problem* is something which I meet, which I find completely before me, but which I can therefore lay siege to and reduce. But a *mystery* is something in which I myself am

---

> involved, and it can therefore only be thought of as a sphere where the distinction between what is in me and what is before me loses its meaning and initial validity." (G. Marcel, *Being and Having* [1949] tr. K. Farrer [Westminster: Dacre Press], p. 117)

Problems are studied by science; mysteries such as the question of being, the nature of the union of body and soul, the "problem of evil," the nature of freedom and love, are the province of philosophy.

Pieper says that insofar as we are animals we inhabit an environment, but as humans we can question the ultimate meaning of the world and its contents. How does this act of questioning occur? To have a "world" or to relate requires a soul, which is to possess an *inwardness* or source of relationships—in short, the capacity to establish and maintain relationships.

There are varying degrees of inwardness or interiority, based on levels of immateriality in being. The principle used here by Pieper is that the *higher the order of a being, the more embracing and wider is its power of establishing relations*: The plant's "world" (relates through "touch" and is capable of nourishment) is narrower than the animal's (relates through sensation, and also capable of locomotion and emotion), and man's is the widest in extension (relating through mind and will, perceiving truth and goodness, having mastery over his acts).

Man possesses what Pieper calls a *spirit* directed towards universal essences ("man," "tree," "justice") and towards infinite truth and goodness (which allows reason to operate scientifically, formulate systems of ethics, and so on). The "isomorphism" between reality and the human mind is possible because the soul is, in a way, "all things," a microcosm of all that is (Aristotle, *On the Soul* III.8). That is, by reason of its immateriality, the soul can receive the forms of things (not the matter—that would be like Goliath, who received the material stone from David's slingshot, and as a consequence died).

> One of Aquinas's favorite axioms is *"that which is received is received according to the mode of the receiver"* (useful for homiletics!).

So, the intellect can "become" what it knows through concepts and reasoning. Knowledge implies a change in the knower (subject) without a change in the known (object). For Pieper, the soul's "silence" means the soul's power to "answer" to the reality of the world left undisturbed.

Discussion Questions:

1. What are some of the characteristics of the "act of philosophizing" according to Pieper, and how does it involve "spirit" and "inwardness"?

2. Why does an animal have an "environment" whereas a person has a "world"? Do you think that Pieper is correct to view *theoria* or speculative philosophy as important in life?

Readings:

*   *PA* Parts II-III

CHAPTER SIX
Christian Philosophy

Philosophy's "ultimate" questions about knowledge, the soul, goodness, and the meaning of life, signal the mind's direction towards infinite being and disconnect the soul from the complacent, bourgeois familiarity with the "workaday" world. These questions can never be adequately answered in the way one answers the questions of science, since what is being sought by philosophy is not a delimited area of knowledge but the knowledge of the highest cause and a vision of finite things in relation to it.

This is why Pieper agrees with Aquinas that the truth about Being does not belong to us as a possession but rather as a "loan" (*In I Meta.* lectio 3 #64). "Wisdom is the object of philosophy, but as lovingly sought, and never fully possessed." Wonder is a "middle state" between the loving knowledge of "what is" and the final vision of all things in God, a state of joyful hope for that which is not yet fully revealed and which will never be fully comprehended. The philosophical question is thus both a vector towards the plenitude of mystery that is the life of God and a reminder of the fragility of a humanity "on the way" towards happiness.

Fides et Ratio chapter seven details various errors to which philosophy is vulnerable when it ignores its roots in theology and its natural trajectory towards union with God. The dangers of eclecticism (#86), historicism (#87), scientism (#88), pragmatism (#89) and nihilism (#90) hover over the project of philosophies which either refuse to ask the question about transcendence, refuse an answer that is beyond the limits of human reason, or refuse the very possibility of an answer, under the supposition that an answer would infringe on the "purity" of the act of questioning that defines philosophy (e.g. Heidegger, in his refusal to admit any sort of answer to the question "why is there something rather than nothing?").

The tendency to systematize and control reality is seen by Pieper as a powerful intellectual seduction that cuts off the natural impetus behind the act of questioning or the philosophical "drive," for instead of the "turning around" and opening of the soul to the transcendent, the illusion and deception emerges that the human mind masters, even creates, the real. The consequent "despair" lamented by John Paul II is evident in the thought of Nietzsche, for example, whose thought reveals a spiritual agony pushing up from the depths of his "will to power." The spirit's inability to be still and contemplate is evident in Nietzsche's "Night Song":

> This is my loneliness, that I am begirt with light…I do not know
> the happiness of those who receive…this is my poverty…
> (F. Nietzsche, *Thus Spake Zarathustra*,
> tr. M. Cowan [Chicago, 1957], p. 107)

Compare this text with the optimism of St. Augustine's theory of three levels of reality, in which the human will turns itself to happiness that is its gentle weight:

> There is a nature which is susceptible of change and with respect
> to both place and time, namely, the corporeal. There is another
> nature which is in no way susceptible of change with respect to
> place, but only with respect to time, namely, the spiritual. And
> there is a third Nature which can be changed neither in respect to

102

place nor in respect to time: that is, God...The highest is essential blessedness; the lowest, that which cannot be either blessed or wretched, and the intermediate nature lives in wretchedness when it stoops towards that which is lowest, and in blessedness when it turns towards that which is highest....

(St. Augustine, *Letter* 18, to Coelestinus)

Turning to God in gratitude is the prelude to living in communion with others. In this vein, Pope Benedict XVI linked love, contemplation, and the conformity to Christ as the condition for authentic self-gift in *Deus Caritas Est* #7: "Anyone who wishes to give love must also receive love as a gift...Yet to become such a source, one must constantly drink anew from the original source, which is Jesus Christ, from whose pierced heart flows the love of God." Hence the Dominican ideal proposed by Aquinas—*contemplata aliis tradere* (*ST* III 40.1 ad 2: "passing on the fruits of one's contemplation"). Only through contemplation can we meet the needs of others and make them our own, says Pope Benedict XVI.

So the "totality" to which the human soul is open is not limited to the feeble products of the human mind. It is more a marvelous miscellany than a catalogue of data, a sort of living symbiosis of the truths of philosophy and faith in which the benefits are mutual. Plato's perception of the link between *eros,* the universal search for wholeness, and the philosopher's quest for truth is revealed in Aristophanes' myth in the *Symposium*—a sign that the Greeks knew the dependence of philosophy on theology.

The Christian philosopher is less concerned with defending the "turf" or "purity" of either philosophy or theology (although he clearly distinguishes their methods, starting points and goals) than with entertaining evidence and explanatory power from any rational quarter. This interaction between disciplines is a delicate "counterpoint" (Pieper) that presents arguments without destroying the mystery at the heart of things.

Therefore, "Christian philosophy" is not a contradiction but a graceful awareness that considers ultimate questions according to two lights: a) human experience and reason; b) the hints or suggestions inspired by faith (e.g. concept of "person" from the nature of God, the concept of "happiness" from beatitude, the value of individual persons from divine providence). The diagram below illustrates the various types of knowledge and how they relate to one another:

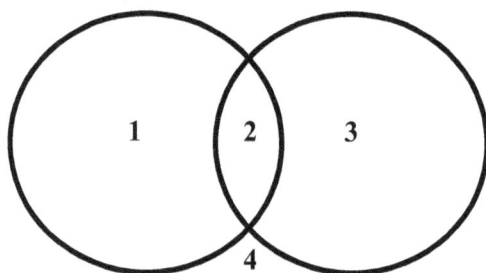

1. the *articles of faith*: revealed, indemonstrable truths (God as Trinity, Incarnation…)
2. the *preambles of faith* (*praeambula fidei*): revealed truths that are demonstrable through philosophy (God's existence, His qualities, problems in philosophy of religion). Why do these need to be revealed and not just left to demonstration? Since many lack the time, inclination and ability to grasp them, and often do so with some degree of error
3. *nonrevealed* philosophical truths about anything—(human happiness, the virtues, the soul, the nature of knowledge, free will…)
4. *scientific & commonsense* truths (definition of light/gravity; proverbs)

Christian philosophy as practiced in all its richness by Pieper is reflected in the creative syntheses of Popes John Paul II and Benedict XVI and in the theory of natural law expounded by Aquinas discussed in Part

Two. Man's freedom is, as Pope John Paul II says, "patterned on God's freedom," which guarantees human dignity by our obedience to the divine law (*Veritatis Splendor* #42). Our free obedience to God's law constitutes what he calls a "participated theonomy," in that our reason and will share in God's wisdom and providence. For St. Thomas, the rational creature is subject to Divine Providence in "the most excellent way... by being provident both for itself, and for others...it has a share of the Eternal Reason" (*ST* I-II 91.2). The God who keeps an order in things by sweetly disposing forms to their inclinations and ends, belies the atheist claim that Christians hold to a coercive ethical "heteronomy" in which we are subjected to an omnipotent, absolute, arbitrary and intolerant Will (*Veritatis Splendor* #41). Rather, authentic freedom is related to an objective good, which is established by Divine Wisdom ordering every being towards its end (*Veritatis Splendor* #71).

The dovetailing of natural and supernatural wisdoms discerned by Pieper is possible, in the end, only because the light of natural reason is the reflection in man of the splendor of God's countenance. And in this recognition Pieper, inspired by St. Thomas, leads us towards the feast of abundance in God's house, where we will see light within the divine light (Ps. 36.8-9).

Discussion Questions:

1. Why do Pieper and St. Thomas say that wisdom can be lovingly sought, but never fully "possessed"? Do you agree, and do you think that this fact diminishes the value of our efforts at philosophy?

2. What are some of the advantages of "Christian philosophy" in comparison to philosophies that deny faith? How do you think Pope John Paul II (and Pope Benedict XVI) would connect Christian philosophy to the search for happiness?

Readings:

- *PA* Part IV

CONCLUSION

In walking the way towards happiness, we have found that Greek philosophers, no less than Christian thinkers, affirm the universal, timeless quality of our desire for a comprehensive form of flourishing made possible in part by our acts of knowledge and love.

Aristotle taught us about human fulfilment in a way that accents our rationality and our teleological or end-directed nature. For him, we find our happiness in both the moral and ontological senses only through a well-chosen life of self-actualizing virtue which binds our soul to its highest good and to others in the community of friendship. In furnishing St. Thomas Aquinas with the foundations of a rich realist metaphysics and the lineaments of a theory of natural law, the Philosopher's thought passed into Christian streams. It shaped the profound Thomist meditations of Josef Pieper, engaging the world of modern philosophy and culture. Pope John Paul II's magisterial works on faith, morality, and philosophy also assimilated, adapted and artfully deployed the Thomist genius for the life of the Church.

The notes of spiritual activity, of virtue as a habit which perfects our appetites, passions, and emotions, and of the soul's reach towards permanence and transcendence, combine to characterize the Thomist view of happiness as heavily indebted to the Greek mind. But because Aristotle's eudaimonism was the work of limited human reason, its focus was on human acts, and could not fully encompass the truth that man is *capax Dei*, that is to say, radically open to God.

But when the acts of man are the fruit of the Holy Spirit, they proceed, according to St. Thomas, from a "divine sowing" and blossom as flowers of the spiritual life, reaching towards our ultimate end—eternal life (*ST* I-II 70.1 ad 1). As Spirit, Love, and Gift, God draws us towards Himself according to the law of divine liberty, by which we gain in freedom in proportion to yielding our reason and desires to His purifying, elevating and illuminating influence.

Under the aegis of grace, we conform ourselves to God and come to share in His inner life through the theological virtues of faith, hope and charity, which are strengthened by the Spirit's Gifts. As rational creatures, we have a unique call to live above the condition of our human nature and to participate in the divine good (*ST* I-II 110.1). This occurs by means of acts flowing forth from God Himself within us, saturating our souls in both holy transcendence and humble interiority. This amazing truth is possible because as Love Itself, God gives *Himself* to us as His first Gift (*Contra Gentiles* IV.21).

St. Thomas's Christian philosophy of happiness superseded Aristotle's noble pagan theory in three ways. First, the Christian participates in (and does not merely imitate) divine blessedness, through friendship with God. Second, the Christian responds to God's initiative through grace, which makes the virtuous life possible. Third, our happiness is not only partly forged from the tragedies of life (as it is for Aristotle), but is entirely grounded in Christ, the object of our beatitude. In redeeming creation through the mysteries of the Incarnation, Passion, and Resurrection, He transfigures our weakness through His salvific power and sacrificial love. With burning gold, his crown of pain subdues our rebellious hearts and makes them free for love, thus setting our mind on its proper task of pursuing truth within His ways.

THE PATH OF SPIRITUAL HAPPINESS

So, as Pope John Paul II persuasively argued, faith strengthens and purifies human reason and emboldens philosophy to investigate and contemplate reality in its full complexity and depth. In its turn, Christian philosophy directs our freedom to its proper home in Truth, through which culture is vivified, and the common good is promoted. For the Christian philosopher, our humanity is not so much a yoke or prison which burdens our soul as much as it is the pinions by which it flies from worldly caverns to its true celestial home.

Josef Pieper's philosophical exhortations hasten us further along the path to spiritual happiness. His vision both reinforces Aristotle's and Aquinas's view of the intellect's comprehensive, contemplative power and scope, and anticipates Pope John Paul II's expression of the harmonic unity of faith and reason and its healing effects on culture. The intuitive and contemplative sources of authentic leisure tie man to God through transcendent acts such as Christian philosophy and worship, in a festivity that celebrates the gratuitous nature of divine love, leading us to true happiness.

Given modern philosophy's night dreams of deafening dread that have shattered Western culture by shrouding the Greek image of truth from the ordinary mind and by driving the feast of charity from the town square into the desert, only the witness of Christians joined together in philosophical communion can now begin to shape us to His ends, beyond our own. It is difficult to know the invisible, but Pieper's philosophy proves most useful in our times, an apparent decline of day. His Thomism is as welcome as morning dew on the parched grass, inviting our gratitude that heaven's glory has been pitched in our camp of death. God Himself, not the work of our hands, has lit our entry into His immeasurable joy.

We have reason for our lofty hope, since our eyes have beheld some signs of the sweetness that lies ahead. Beatitude is not an illusion conceived from the whirlwind of frail human desires. Nor is it a separate realm of individualism and pride borne from the rush and cacophony of competing philosophical systems, lamented so poignantly by Pope John Paul II.

It is only by being struck with wonder at the depth of being that our reason learns to bow its crest before the wilderness of contemplation, and find there the mountain of divine truth and power whose streams alone can renew and refresh a weary civilization. As Christians who philosophize, we should all yearn for the joy of such a life, whose light runs through our spirit's veins as blood within our bodies and as God's entwining love chases us through the passage of our days and years.

GLOSSARY
Part One

dualism—the view that reality (and the human being) is made up of two irreducible, opposed elements of matter and spirit

end (*telos*)—the goal of a certain activity

Form / Idea—an eternal pattern or model that is the cause of the physical being corresponding to it (Plato)

form / nature of a thing—the principle of life and intelligibility in a thing; that which makes it the type of thing that it is (Aristotle)

good (in general)—that which is desired, aimed at, or chosen as an end or a means to an end;

    a) real vs. apparent good:

        real good—that which is actually good, as fulfilling a thing's nature

        apparent good—that which seems good to a subject

    b) moral vs. metaphysical good:

        moral good—that which is virtuous and helps us attain happiness

        metaphysical good—the thing having everything necessary for its nature to function

habit—a disposition acquired by repetition

happiness—virtuous activity of the soul throughout life (includes moral and intellectual virtue)

hedonism—the view that pleasure is the only and ultimate view in life

hylemorphism—the view that the human person is a unity composed of matter (*hyle*) and an organizing life principle (*morphe*) (Aristotle)

mean—the middle between two extremes

need vs. **want**

    need—something required for a nature to function

    want—something desired but not necessary

philosophy—love of wisdom (*philo-sophia*); the science that seeks to understand all things by knowing their causes by human reason

practical wisdom—knowing how to deliberate well about our final end and about the means to that end

reason—a) **speculative reason**: mind seeking the truth for its own sake; b) **practical reason**: reason as applied to action; c) **productive reason**: reason as applied to making

virtue—a good habit; an excellence

    intellectual virtue—perfection of the mind in its acts of speculative, practical, and productive reason

    moral virtue—the habit of right desire (a characteristic involving choice, consisting in observing the mean)

will—rational appetite; the power of the soul to desire or choose a good known by the mind

GLOSSARY
Part Two

appetite—an inclination or tendency to some good or suitable object

    will—rational appetite in man for his proper good, viz., happiness

beatitude—supernatural and perfect happiness belonging to nature elevated by sanctifying grace and the light of glory to the eternal vision of God

charity (*caritas*)—the infused supernatural virtue whereby one loves God above all things for His own sake and one's neighbours for the sake of God; friendship with God.

happiness—satisfaction of desire in possessing its true and proper good

    imperfect happiness—fulfillment of our natural powers here on earth (corresponds to pagan/Aristotelian "natural" happiness), involving external, bodily and spiritual goods

    perfect happiness—possession and enjoyment of God as our ultimate, supernatural, and heavenly end in the beatific vision (beatitude)

human acts—acts that flow from reason and free will, subject to moral evaluation as morally good or evil

    acts of man—morally neutral or irrelevant actions performed by humans

love (*amor*)—the primary perfection of the appetitive powers (both sensory and rational): the movement of the appetite towards a good; the proportion (*proportio*) that exists between a being and its good. The origin of *desire* (when the loved good is not yet possessed) and *delight* or *joy* (when the good *is* possessed)

love of concupiscence—the will's motion towards the good(s) willed for a person

love of friendship—the will's motion towards the person who is loved; love in the most perfect sense, basis of "love of concupiscence"

passions—motions of the sense appetites tending towards the attainment of some real or apparent good, or the avoidance of some evil; in general terms, "being acted upon by another"

philosophy—love of wisdom (*philo-sophia*) (starting point is data of experience and natural reason; goal is naturally known truths about God)

prudence—the intellectual virtue of practical wisdom, the knowledge of choosing good means to proper ends

theology—scientific, speculative study of God, both in Himself and in relation to creation (starting point is *revealed truths* about God; goal is salvation)

virtue—good habit perfecting rational powers (*intellectual virtue*) and appetite (*moral virtue*) to act according to the rule of reason; a habit making its possessor and his actions good

> **acquired virtue**—natural virtue whose principle, object and end is man
>
> **cardinal virtues**—four virtues on which "hinge" the rest of the moral life (*prudence, justice, temperance, fortitude)*
>
> **supernatural/infused virtue**—virtue whose principle and end is God; given by grace and not acquired by human effort; "a good quality of the mind by which we live righteously, of which no one makes bad use, which God works in us without us" (St. Augustine)
>
> **theological virtue**—a good infused habit whose object is God (*faith, hope, charity)*

GLOSSARY
Part Three

Christian philosophy—philosophy that considers ultimate questions according to the light and methods of natural reason but also with the guiding questions of faith. The concrete project of the philosopher who believes and thinks about being in its relation to mystery

contemplation—pursuit of truth for its own sake rather than for its utility. One of three levels of intellectual vision: natural, revealed, or mystical. The "silent perception of reality" attained through intuition (Pieper)

ecstasy—state of being "outside" oneself through contemplation or rapture; rising above the workaday world and accessing mystery through worship

incommensurable activities—activities that are not reducible to other ones, such as worship, philosophy, etc.

inwardness—the capacity to establish and maintain relationships

leisure—the foundation of Western culture that is grounded in divine worship; Greek *skole*. The gate to the experience of superhuman, lifegiving existential forces (Pieper) and the condition of humanising activities such as contemplation and the liberal arts

Liberal arts—activities practiced by "freemen" that concern immaterial realities (literature, arts, philosophy, etc.) and enjoys them as "ends"
  servile arts—material skills necessary to produce the necessities of life

the philosophical act—to transcend or step outside the world of work and utility and receptively contemplate reality; to wonder

philosophy—the love of wisdom and the openness to the totality of being as a mysterious gift. The incomplete and human pursuit of wisdom that begins in wonder and is structured by hope

"problem" (Marcel)—a puzzle or question soluble by reason
  vs. "mystery"—a reality in which we participate through intuition and love but which can never be fully comprehended

rationalism—philosophical theory that reduces the truth value of statements to the findings of reason alone, without recourse to the data of faith; refers to "closed systems" of some philosophers and scientists

spirit—the capacity to relate to the "totality" of being; characteristic of the human being

transcendent activities—nonutilitarian acts that connect us to the mystery of existence, such as philosophy, the arts, and moments of existential shock (love, death) that reveal our radical dependence and contingence, and inspire gratitude

wonder—the state that characterizes philosophy, as between the loving knowledge of "what is" and the final vision of all things in God; a turning towards the true, the good and the beautiful in an act of gratitude and hope

workaday world—the utilitarian world of work whose goal is the satisfaction of material needs; often misidentified as the "common good" of society. It can lead to the ideal of the "worker" with the traits of excessive activity, toil and the reduction of life to its "social function"

world—range or field of relationships a thing has

    vs. **environment**—sphere of material needs a thing has

worship—the core of celebration as the affirmation of the universe and the experience of reality in a transcendent way through special space and time, sacrifice and sacrament; the festival celebrating God's gift of being that is accompanied by gratitude and joy. The foundation of leisure and the transcendent activities that constitute culture

RECOMMENDED READINGS

Aristotle. *Nicomachean Ethics,* translated by W.D. Ross, in Richard McKeon, editor, *The Basic Works of Aristotle.* New York: Random House, 1941.

Plato, *Phaedo,* translated by Hugh Tredennick in *Plato: The Collected Dialogues,* edited by Edith Hamilton and Huntingdon Cairnes. Princeton, New Jersey: Princeton University Press, 1961.

St. Thomas Aquinas. *Summa Theologica,* translated by Anton C. Pegis, in Anton C. Pegis, editor, *Basic Writings of St. Thomas Aquinas,* Volumes 1 and 2. New York: Random House, 1945.

Josef Pieper. *Leisure: The Basis of Culture* (includes *The Philosophical Act*), translated by Alexander Dru. San Francisco: Ignatius Press, 2009. English translation 1963 (original German edition 1952).

Josef Pieper. *Happiness and Contemplation,* translated by Richard and Clara Winston. South Bend, Indiana: St. Augustine's Press, 1998. English translation 1958 (original German edition 1979).

Josef Pieper. *A Guide to St. Thomas Aquinas,* translated by Richard and Clara Winston. San Francisco: Ignatius Press, 1991 (original German edition 1986).

Pope John Paul II. *Fides et Ratio/Faith and Reason.* Vatican City: Libreria Editrice Vaticana, 1998.

Pope John Paul II. *Veritatis Splendor/On the Splendor of Truth.* Vatican City: Libreria Editrice Vaticana, 1993.

Pope Benedict XVI. *Deus Caritas Est/God is Love.* Vatican City: Libreria Editrice Vaticana, 1995.

Joseph Owens. *Human Destiny: Some Problems for Catholic Philosophy.* Washington, D.C.: Catholic University of America Press, 1985.

Etienne Gilson. *The Christian Philosophy of St. Thomas Aquinas,* 5th edition, translated by L. K. Shook. New York: Random House, 1956 (original French 5th edition: 1948).

Mortimer Adler. *Aristotle for Everybody: Difficult Thought Made Easy.* New York: Macmillan, 1978.

www.ingramcontent.com/pod-product-compliance
Lightning Source LLC
Chambersburg PA
CBHW022032090426
42741CB00007B/1035